Olympiad 1936: blaze of glory for Hitler's Reich

Judith Holmes

Editor-in-Chief: Barrie Pitt
Editor: David Mason
Art Director: Sarah Kingham
Picture Editor: Robert Hunt
Designer: David A Evans
Cover: Denis Piper
Photographic Research: Cairine Cameron
Cartographer: Richard Natkiel

Photographs for this book were specially selected from the following Archives: from left to right pages; 4–5 Ullstein; 7 US Library of Congress; 9 US National Archives; 10 Ullstein; 11 British Olympic Association; 12 US National Archives; 12–16 Ullstein; 18 Suddeutscher Verlag; 19 Ullstein; 20 British Olympic Association; 21 Ullstein; 23 British Olympic Association; 24–25 Ullstein; 25 US National Archives; 26–27 Ullstein; 28–29 British Olympic Association; 30 Suddeutscher Verlag; 32–33 Ullstein; 34 Roger Viollet; 35 US National Archives; 35 Keystone; 36 Radio Times Hulton; 38–40 British Olympic Association; 41 Keystone; 42–43 Ullstein; 44–45 Fox; 47 Popperfoto; 49 Radio Times Hulton; 50–51 Ullstein; 52–53 US National Archives; 54 British Olympic Association; 55 US Library of Congress; 56 British Olympic Association; 57 US Library of Congress; 58–61 Ullstein; 60 US Library of Congress; 61 Ullstein; 62 US National Archives; 63 British Olympic Association; 64 Ullstein; 65 US Library of Congress; 66 US National Archives; 67 British Olympic Association; 68–69 Suddeutscher Verlag; 70–73 US National Archives; 74–77 British Olympic Association; 78–81 US National Archives; 82–83 Suddeutscher Verlag; 82–83 British Olympic Association; 84–85 Ullstein; 84 Suddeutscher Verlag; 85–86 Ullstein; 87 US Library of Congress; 88 Ullstein; 90–91 Suddeutscher Verlag; 92 Ullstein; 94–95 British Olympic Association; 96–97 Ullstein; 98 US Library of Congress; 99 Suddeutscher Verlag; 101 Ullstein; 102–103 US Library of Congress; 106 Ullstein; 107 Suddeutscher Verlag; 108–111 British Olympic Association; 112–117 Ullstein; 120 US National Archives; 121–123 Ullstein; 123 US Library of Congress; 124–126 British Olympic Association; 128–129 US Library of Congress; 130 Ullstein; 131 US National Archives; 131–135 British Olympic Association; 134 Ullstein; 134–135 British Olympic Association; 136 US Library of Congress; 136–137 British Olympic Association; 139 Ullstein; 140–143 Suddeutscher Verlag; 143 Ullstein; 144–145 Bundesarchiv; 146 Ullstein; 149 Suddeutscher Verlag; 151 US National Archives; 153 British Olympic Association; 154 Ullstein; 156–157 British Olympic Association; 159 Ullstein; Front Cover: Bundesarchiv; Back Cover: Ullstein

First Printing: November 1971
Printed in United States of America

Ballantine Books Inc.
101 Fifth Avenue New York NY 10003

An Intext Publisher

Contents

Politics in sport

Introduction by Sydney L Mayer

Politics and sport have become inseparable. When the ex-heavyweight boxing champion, Mohammed Ali, a Black Muslim, tours Africa and the Middle East, this fact is more than apparent. The controversies in England about playing cricket with white South Africans; the refusal of South Africa to allow Arthur Ashe to play tennis in their country; Ashe's counter-statements regarding the treatment of blacks south of the Zambesi; going back a bit further, the struggle of Jackie Robinson, the first black baseball player in the major leagues, to gain acceptance, and his involvement in party political struggles in America subsequently; all of these are examples of politics influencing sport and sports figures involved in political arguments.

This has not always been the case. When the Olympic Games were revived in Athens in 1896, despite the intra-European power struggles that involved every participating state at the first modern Olympiad, these rivalries were sublimated to the cause of sport, fair play and camaraderie among the athletes, French and German, English and Russian alike. Although the Olympic Games were suspended during the First World War, they were revived soon after, and the principles which motivated their revival continued. When the Olympics were held in Amsterdam and Los Angeles during the inter-war period, politics were forced once again to take a back seat to sportsmanship.

One motivation for deciding to hold the 1936 Olympiad in Berlin was to indicate to the world that the defeated great power in the Great War was again accepted by all nations. But between the time it was decided to hold the next Olympics in Germany and the time the Games were opened, Adolf Hitler came to power and soon eliminated most aspects of the democratic Weimar Republic which accepted the invitation to the Games in the first place. There were some misgivings about staging the next Olympiad in Nazi Germany, but in the interests of keeping politics out of sport, the International Olympic Committee decided not to change its plans, despite the protests of Jewish and left-wing organizations which were (reasonably enough) opposed to the Third Reich from the outset.

Hitler, however, intended to stage more than merely a great athletic contest.

He knew that the eyes of the world would be focussed on his régime, and millions of marks were spent to make certain that the participants were better housed, fed and entertained than in any previous Olympiad. In large measure Hitler was successful in staging a dramatic and exciting spectacle. But all of this was in aid of propaganda for the Third Reich. Films and radio were to spread the tales of wealth and success and full employment within the Third Reich to the depression-ridden world of the west. Lavish parades and speeches by Hitler and Goebbels were to punctuate the sporting events at Berlin's Sportspalast and other sporting sites. The Nazi propaganda machine was made to work overtime. It wanted to show the world that not only was Germany again a great power, that it was the happiest, richest country in the world despite the jealousies of her rivals – Hitler wanted to indicate that the Aryan race, particularly the Germans, were physically superior to inferior breeds. And although the German team did well in the Games, the spotlight shifted from Hitler to the exploits of Jesse Owens and other black, and 'non-Aryan', athletes to point up the fact that Aryan racial supremacy was a myth. The Nazi propaganda machine did what it could to play down the black victories, to point out the fact that even half-Jews were glad to participate on the German team. In short, Hitler made sport an arm of political propaganda to an extent that had never before been attempted.

Judith Holmes discusses the 1936 Olympiad, the anti-Olympics that were held in protest against it, the thrilling sporting events and good sportsmanship of the athletes who carried on the Olympic tradition, as well as the propaganda which the Third Reich made of the Berlin Games. Her narrative and the events which followed after the Games were a memory make it abundantly clear that politics and sport were made inseparable by Hitler. Neither the Olympic Games nor any other major international sporting event after 1936 could ever be free from the uses various governments or interest groups would make of them. Perhaps the black athletes who raised their arms in the Black Power salute at the 1968 Olympiad in Mexico City had more in common with Hitler and Goebbels than they ever imagined.

Hitler prepares

In 1932 Herbert Hoover, immersed in his battle with Franklin Delano Roosevelt over the forthcoming presidential elections, declined an invitation to open the Olympic Games at Los Angeles; he was too busy with politics to bother about sport! This was the last time a politician could automatically make such a distinction; from that time on, for good or ill, politics and international sport would be irrevocably linked.

On 26th May 1930 the members of the Olympic Congress gathered at Berlin University to hear Germany's request that the XI Olympic Games be held in Berlin in 1936; they can have had no idea of the world-shattering events that would take place before that time, nor of the far-reaching repercussions their eventual decision would have. For the XI Games were not only record breakers in the sports world; for the first time ever, politics would affect international sport. For the first time the Olympic Games would be deliberately used,

with consummate skill and efficiency, as propaganda for the government of the host country and for the first time people all over the world would object to their country's participation on moral grounds, out of disgust for the politics of the host country involved. 'Unthinkable!' would have been the reaction of those sportsmen gathered at Berlin; but it happened, and was to continue happening as late as 1970, when the battle over South Africa's participation in international sport was being waged as bitterly and with the same philosophical positions as was the conflict over the 'Nazi Olympic Games'.

But even in those early days of 1930 the seeds that were to produce the controversies and complications of 1936 had already been sown. As early as 1920, while Germany smarted under the indignity of defeat and the 'war

Werner March discusses the model of the renovation of the Grunewald Stadium, Berlin, with Dr Diem

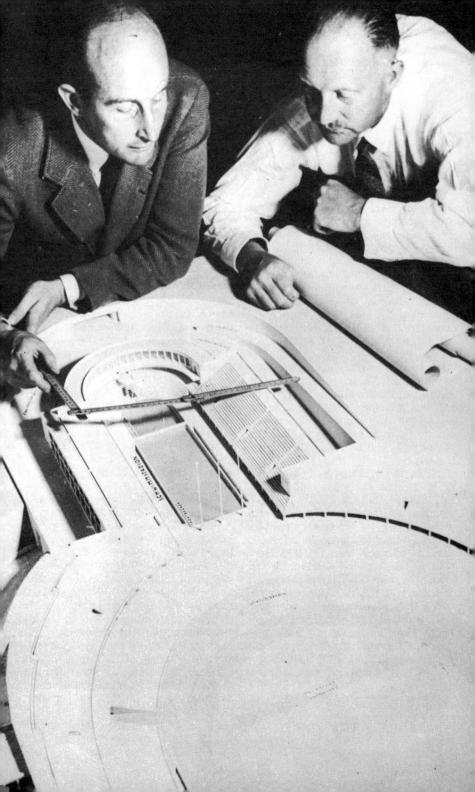

guilt clause' of the Treaty of Versailles, pressure from the Right threatened the new Weimar Republic. The Communists in Germany reacted strongly to this threat and soon the German people were moving more and more towards the two extremes. When in 1921 the Allies presented their enormous bill for reparations there were angry demands that Germany refuse to pay; the moderates' realization that the threat of invasion made this impossible led only to more resentment. When Poland was awarded part of the rich coal district of Upper Silesia bitterness was increased. By this time Adolf Hitler was well on his road to power; he was already the leader of the Nazi Party, though in 1922 it was still a very minor political force. Attempts by the moderates to meet the increasing threat from the Right were largely nullified by the growing inflation of 1922-23. France's occupation of the Ruhr in 1923 and Germany's subsequent passive resistance made matters worse. The middle classes, ruined by the inflation, could not bring themselves to support either the Nazi or Communist Parties. Instead they placed their hopes on the moderate parties.

By 1925 the inflation had ended and the moderates had made some gains. The Dawes Plan, which called for French evacuation of the Ruhr and a revised scale of reparations, was accepted (over the protests of most Germans who considered it a sinister attempt to enslave Germany to foreign masters) and Germany signed the Locarno Pact. In 1926 she was admitted to the League of Nations and in 1928 was a signatory to the Kellogg-Briand Pact which outlawed aggressive war forever. The Young Plan reduced reparations still further and in June, 1930, the Allies evacuated the Rhineland – five years ahead of schedule. Many of these German gains, however, had been accomplished with so much difficulty that they did not improve the temper of

March was the architect employed by the German Olympic Organising Committee to remodel Grunewald so that it could accomodate more people and be a fitting show place

the German people; furthermore, by 1930 Germany was in the throes of the Great Depression, and the middle classes, who had just begun to recover from the inflation of 1922-23, found themselves ruined again. The Nazis gained more recruits than ever, and in the elections of September 1930 were to increase their representation in the Reichstag from 12 to 107 seats.

Political and economic upheavals notwithstanding, work on the Olympic Games proceeded. The Reich Commission for Physical Training was placed in charge of the preparations and the architect Werner March drew up his plans for remodelling the Grunewald Stadium in Berlin. As the German Organizing Committee felt that 'the festive character of former Olympic Games had left much to be desired', Dr Diem, Secretary-General of the Committee, immediately began work on a Festival Play to be presented at the Games.

By the time the International Olympic Committee held its next

meeting in Barcelona on 25th April 1931, Germany's plans were well organized and Dr Lewald was able to give a spirited presentation of Germany's claim. He showed the Committee March's plans for the renovation of Grunewald Stadium and argued that Berlin, situated as it was in the heart of Europe, was the ideal spot for the Games. He also pointed out that Germany had been awarded the Olympic Games scheduled for 1916; since they had never been held she deserved another chance. No Spanish delegates had managed to come to the meeting and general attendence was poor due to political unrest in Spain. When the votes were cast forty-three went to Berlin, and sixteen to Barcelona, the other leading contender, with eighty abstentions. Since so many delegates were missing a poll was taken of the absentees by mail, and it was not until 13th May 1931 that the XI Olympic Games were officially awarded to Berlin. Germany's goals at this time were

The departmental directors of the German Organising Committee keep fit for the herculean task of organising the XI Olympic Games. In the center is Dr Diem, Secretary-General of the committee. On the right is Bill Henry, Sports Director of the X Olympic Games, held in Los Angeles in 1932

summed up in a report issued by the Reich Commission for Physical Training a week later: 'These Games are the expression of a new outlook and a new youth. The world expects the German Nation to organize and present this Festival in an exemplary manner, emphasizing at the same time its moral and artistic aspects. All forces must be exerted for the advancement of the Olympic ideals and the honor of Germany.' But by 1936 the Games would not express the outlook of the Weimar Republic; instead the philosophy and youth of Nazi Germany under the aegis of Hitler would be the guiding force.

An organizing committee was duly

formed and soon (by August 1931) a model of the new stadium was placed on exhibition in Berlin. But the committee members soon found that Germany in 1931 was not the best place to raise the vast amounts of money needed for their enterprise. There were 5,000,000 wage earners out of work; the middle classes were facing ruin; farmers were unable to meet their mortgage payments; the Reichstag was paralysed, the government was floundering, and President Hindenburg, at 84, was sinking into senility.

The depression deepened further when Heinrich Brüning's plan for a customs union with Austria was vetoed by the World Court at the instigation of the Allied Powers, and by the collapse of the great Austrian bank, the *Kredit Anstalt*. Politically the Weimar Republic was in its

Dr Theodor Lewald, Secretary-General of the German Committee before Diem. His international friendships were generally credited as winning the prize of the XI Olympics for Berlin, but in 1933 he was removed from his post because it was revealed that he was a *Mischling* – his paternal grandmother had been born a Jew

death throes. Hitler won the support of Fritz Thyssen and other coal and steel magnates, thus gaining sound financial backing in addition to his mass following. Although some Nazis believed the time was ripe for a *putsch*, Hitler declined, for he believed he could gain power legally, and in March 1932 he ran against Hindenburg for the Presidency. He lost by a relatively narrow margin, and despite efforts to suppress them the Nazis scored impressive victories in the local elections that followed. In May Hindenburg forced Brüning to resign and in his place appointed Franz von Papen, an extreme right-winger. Papen succeeded in freeing Germany from her reparations payments and in July called for new elections. After they had been held he was unpleasantly surprised to find that the Nazis were now the largest single party in the Reichstag; he tried to compromise with them by taking a few into the government, but Hitler would settle only for the Chancellorship.

Hindenburg refused to hear of this, so Papen decided to call yet another election. The increased pressure took its toll; at the same time Papen brought his influence to bear on Hitler's financial supporters, so that the party's funds became dangerously low. In November the Nazis' representation fell from 230 to 196 seats.

At this point Papen could probably have kept Hitler from power; however, due to his own lack of support in the Reichstag he was forced to resign. Kurt von Schleicher, who had engineered Papen's appointment, thus seriously weakening the government as well as making it more unpopular, found himself forced into the Chancellorship, making a last-ditch effort to save the Republic. He succeeded only in alienating almost everyone, and in January 1933 he was forced to resign. Hindenburg was persuaded to appoint Hitler to the Chancellorship; 30th January 1933, the day of his appointment, sounded the death knell of the Weimar Republic.

The model of the new stadium. It was placed on exhibition in Berlin in 1933 in order to raise money for the Organising Committee in depression-ridden Germany

Obviously, in times as troubled as these, sport must take second place in the public eye, and the Organizing Committee found money very hard to come by, especially since they were determined to get enough not only to present the XI Games in Germany, but to be represented at the Games in Los Angeles in 1932 as well, for it was felt that it was necessary to benefit from the experience of a visit to the leading sporting nation of the world. The necessary money was finally gathered together from a variety of sources; in addition to voluntary contributions and a grant of 1,000,000 Reichmarks from the Reich Post Ministry, funds were raised by means of special postage stamps, a national lottery, and the 'Olympic Penny' – an extra charge added to the price of admission to all sporting events. Their goal attained, the Committee set off for Los Angeles. The organization of the X Olympic Games was studied with great care, especially the Olympic Village – the first in the history of the Games – and in November 1932 the Committee returned to Germany to set up their organizational outline.

When Hitler came to power two months later he took immediate steps to transform his Chancellorship into a dictatorship. Since the Nazis and the Nationalists still lacked a majority in the Reichstag he tricked the leader of the Center Party, Monsignor Kaas, into agreeing to hold new elections on 5th March. With all the resources of the government behind them the Nazis were able to launch a huge campaign, but it soon became obvious that something sensational would be needed to convince a public which remained unreasonably sceptical. The sensation obligingly appeared on 27th February when the Reichstag was set on fire – according to Hitler, by the Communists, although today it is certain that this theory is false. Despite their efforts the Nazis managed to corner only 44% of the vote. However, by the simple expedients of banning the Communist Party delegates, arresting as many Social Democrats as necessary and filling the hall with storm troopers, Hitler managed to get the famous 'Enabling Act' passed on 23rd March by the necessary two-thirds majority. The Reichstag had dug its own grave and obligingly jumped in. Though it would continue to meet throughout the Third Reich, it would henceforth serve only as a sounding board for Hitler's pronouncements.

In April the Ministry of Propaganda was formed under Goebbels, and the various state governments were stripped of their powers, making Germany a highly centralized state. Upon the death of Hindenburg in August, Hitler assumed the title of President as well as Chancellor, although he preferred to be called *Der Führer*. Other political parties were suppressed. Many Germans were happy to have a strong man at the helm after the ineffectual intrigue-ridden governments of the Weimar Republic. After the 'blood purge' in 1934 – the infamous 'night of the long knives' when Röhm, other SA officers and miscellaneous political opponents were assassinated – Hitler's position both within his own party and in Germany was secure. Jews in Germany became targets within a few days of the passage of the Enabling Act. Their businesses and professions were boycotted and their persons were subject to attack with impunity. In May 1933 Germany was brought before the Council of the League of Nations to answer charges of discrimination in Upper Silesia. Under pressure she agreed to observe the Geneva Convention regarding treatment of minorities in future and to reinstate all 'non-Aryans' who had lost their jobs. Needless to say, this had no effect whatsoever and in September the League protested again – Germany had not reinstated the Jews and in fact persecution had increased. Herr von Keller, the German delegate, made a valiant attempt to reconcile Germany's persecution of her Jewish minority at home with her professed role as 'protector' of German minorities abroad. His arguments were unconvincing in the extreme and the League passed a motion censuring Germany; the censure carried little weight, however, and a month later Germany withdrew from the League altogether. Meanwhile persecution of the Jews continued, as did harassment of Christian churches.

Politics in sport : girls who wanted to marry SS men were required, after Hitler's assumption of power, to possess the Reich sport medal as evidence of their fitness to bear healthy children for the new Reich

Sport, like every other aspect of German life, was affected as well. National Socialism placed great emphasis on physical training, considering that 'physical education develops and forms body and soul . . . through physical exercises rooted in Volkdom'. Girls who wanted to marry SS men were required to possess the Reich sports medal because, as SS Chief Group Leader Jeckeln put it at a meeting of the NSDAP, 'Germany does not need women who can dance beautifully at five o'clock teas, but women who have given proof of their health through accomplishments in the field of sport. The javelin and the springboard are more useful than lipstick in promoting health.' The Hitler Youth movement aimed to bring up young people with strong healthy bodies, faith in their Führer, the future of their country and themselves, and a sense of fellowship that would overcome all social and economic barriers. How well this policy succeeded, at least in physical terms, is pointed up by William L Shirer when he tells how in May 1940 he noted 'the contrast between the German soldiers, bronzed and clean cut from a youth spent in the sunshine on an adequate diet and the first British war prisoners, with their hollow chests, round shoulders, pasty complexions and bad teeth – tragic examples of the youth that England had neglected so irresponsibly between the wars'.

Jews did not fare so well. As early as December 1933 the Jewish Chronicle in London reported that all Jewish sports organizations in Germany with the exception of the Maccabee and the Schild had been disbanded. And of course Jews were excluded from swimming baths, gymnasiums and other places where they might be able to train, So, although the German

Politics in sport : the Hitler Youth movement aimed to raise young people with strong bodies and firm faith in their Führer

Organizing Committee had assured the IOC at Vienna in July that 'in principle' Jews would not be excluded from the German Olympic team, in practice there was very little opportunity for .them to participate. The actual situation was perhaps better expressed by Herr von Tschammer und Osten who was reported by the Associated Press to have said 'We shall see to it that both in our national life and in our relations and competitions with foreign nations only such Germans shall be allowed to represent the nation against whom no objection can be raised.'

Two notable exceptions were to emerge however: Helene Mayer, a German fencing champion, who was partly of Jewish ancestry, was living at the time with her parents in California. In December 1933 she received an invitation to return and fence for Germany in 1936. She finally accepted, after stipulating that she receive full German citizenship. Rudi Ball, an ice hockey champion who was a Jew living outside Germany was invited to come back for the Winter Games at Garmisch-Partenkirchen; he too accepted after some time, amid rumors that his family, still in Germany, had been threatened. He made it plain that he intended leaving Germany immediately after the Games. These two athletes were useful not so much for their contributions to the German team (although Helene Mayer won a silver medal in the Women's Individual Foil competition) as for their propaganda value. Much was made of the fact that Germany, far from discriminating against Jewish athletes, went so far as to recruit German Jews living abroad for her Olympic team.

But if Hitler's rise to power was an immediate disaster for the Jews and a long term disaster for Germany as a whole, it was certainly a godsend for the Organizing Committee. For three years they had had to face not only the problem of raising money in the midst of a depression, but

government indifference and what can only be described as obstructionism on the part of the Berlin city administrators who seemed determined to put every possible obstacle in the path of March's plans for providing facilities for the athletes. But then on 16th March 1933 Dr Lewald paid a visit to the new Chancellor who gave him a most cordial reception. He welcomed the Olympic Games to Berlin, he said, and would do everything possible to ensure their successful presentation. For, he asserted, the Games would contribute substantially to furthering understanding among the nations of the world and would promote the development of sport among German youth – this last being, in his opinion, of vast importance to the welfare of the nation. Lewald also managed to talk to Goebbels who, on 28th March, agreed to form a special commission for dealing with propaganda for the Games.

On 5th October Lewald took Hitler and Wilhelm Frick (Minister for the Interior) on a tour of Grünewald Stadium to point out the proposed renovations. Hitler grew even more enthusiastic and declared that the present plans were inadequate. (Which indeed they were, due to limitations placed on the Committee by the City of Berlin and by their lack of funds.) Instead, he authorized a huge building scheme to be financed out of government funds which ran roughshod over the building restrictions imposed by the city. He declared that 'the Stadium must be erected by the Reich; it will be the task of the nation. If Germany is to stand host to the entire world, her preparations

Helene Mayer, part-Jewish German fencing champion. In a notable exception to the anti-Jewish drift of German policy she was asked to return from California to fence for Germany. She finally accepted after stipulating that she receive full German citizenship

must be complete and magnificent. The exterior of the Stadium must not be of concrete, but of national stone. When a nation has 4,000,000 unemployed it must seek ways and means of providing work for them.' Which last eminently practical point arose out of the same line of reasoning that later led to the establishment of the Works Progress Administration (WPA) and other organizations of a similar nature in America.

Five days later the entire Olympic Committee met with Hitler, Goebbels, Secretary of State Pfundtner and Herr von Keudel, the Commissioner of Woods and Forests. At this time Hitler stated that the New Germany should provide evidence of her cultural accomplishments and ability as well as her prowess in the field of sport. It was decided that official invitations were to be 'artistically designed and reproduced by the Reich

The Reich Sports Minister, Herr von Tschammer und Osten, discusses the Olympic program with Hitler. Tschammer said that 'only such Germans shall be allowed to represent the nation against whom no objection can be raised' – this in effect meant the exclusion of many well qualified Jews

Printing Company', and that the Games would become the responsibility of the entire German nation.

By autumn of 1935 the mould for the Olympic Bell which was to be cast in steel was practically ready for the metal to be poured. It would weigh over 20,000lbs and the rim would bear the words *Ich rufe die Jugend der Welt'* (I Call the Youth of the World). In 1933 the IOC had resolved to make an Olympic Hymn composed by Bradley Keeler official for all time. Dr Lewald, however, had succeeded in obtaining permission for Germany to have her own Olympic hymn in view of 'her great contributions to art and music'. A contest was held in Germany and in August the prize for the best poem was awarded to Robert Lubann. Richard Strauss composed the music and the result is reported to have met with the Führer's hearty approval. In October *Olympic Games 1936*, the official organ of the Olympic Games, reported that although many people had expressed doubts as to whether the Reich Sports Field could be finished on time, these doubts had been finally and definitely settled by the designation of 23rd March 1936 as the official opening day, with ceremonies and a gigantic sporting festival to be staged by the Reich Society for Physical Culture. A suggestion from Alexander Philadelphus, the Director of the Archeological Museum in Athens, that the Olympic Torch be lighted by a lens reflecting

The Olympic Bell. Weighing over 20,000lbs and almost ten feet high, it was inscribed around the rim with 'Ich rufe die Jugend der Welt' (I call the Youth of the World)

the rays of the Olympic sun was incorporated into plans for the preliminary ceremonies.

With all the resources of the government behind it, work towards the Games proceeded apace. At Hitler's request the army 'came to the assistance' of the Organizing Committee and took over the construction of and all arrangements for an Olympic Village – the second to be built in the history of the Games. The Ministry of Propaganda was responsible for publicity, and the Stadium and other facilities were being built with government funds. Lewald and the rest of the Organizing Committee spent a good deal of time trying to convince the IOC and various National Olympic Committees that German politics would not have any bearing on the conduct of the XI Olympic Games.

A fireworks display in Munich greeted the 'Olympic Year'. Garmisch-Partenkirchen, site of the Winter Games scheduled for February, was already decorated with Olympic and Swastika flags and triumphal arches of evergreen. Restaurants had been enlarged and a small village of barracks erected to house administration and press offices. Meanwhile the German Organizing Committee was having trouble with its own internal organization. Herr von Tschammer und Osten, the prominent German sports leader, was reported in a London paper to have made an attempt to oust Dr Lewald from his position as Chairman of the Committee. He failed, but a short time later Hitler appointed him Reich Sports Leader. Five representatives of the Nazi Party were appointed to the Organizing Committee: Group Commander Beckerle, Chief of Staff Lautenbacher representing the Nazi Youth organizations, Standard Commander Nord from the Motor Corps and District Labor Leader Dr Delker of the Nazi Labor Service. The fifth member appointed was Group Commander Reinhardt Heydrich, the long-nosed icy-eyed policeman who was

to become known as 'Hangman' Heydrich before his assassination in Prague in 1942. The *New York Times* noted that from the Nazi point of view these would not be considered 'political' appointments, since the party in power was not just a political party, but represented all of Germany.

By 7th January all the seats for track and field events in the Summer Games had been sold, and now the main problem confronting the organizers was that of international public opinion. Early in January Hitler issued a categoric order that all anti-Jewish boycott posters and banners must go. *Der Stürmer*, the notorious weekly edited by Julius Streicher that concentrated on pornographic tales of Jewish sexual crimes and whose obscenity disgusted even many Nazis, must not appear on the streets; even the *Stürmerkasten*, the boxes in which it was displayed, were to disappear. These orders were backed up by a flood of directives from the Ministry of Propaganda and other government sources. On 23rd January Frick – with what one American newspaper called 'perhaps unexpected tact' – requested that sports clothes, not uniforms, be worn at the Winter Games and also warned the guests of honor that they were to leave their large retinues of adjutants at home. He ended his memorandum with a reminder that the IOC and GOC were solely responsible for the manner in which events at the Games were to be carried through.

A circular was issued by the authorities at Bad Tölz which was marked 'Strictly Confidential' and read: 'To all restaurants and larger hotels. Bad Tölz like other places will, on the occasion of the Olympic Games, be visited by a number of foreigners who, unfortunately, will have a false conception of the New Germany. The restaurant and hotel industry thus takes up a prominent position in this year of foreign visits. Foreign visitors must be convinced that Germany's hospitality cannot be surpassed by

A model of the Olympic Village, the second to be built in the history of the Games. It was constructed by the German army

any other country. In conjunction with the political leadership we therefore ask you to handle the Jewish question in a suitable manner.'

The press was warned that they must not publish any reports on clashes with foreigners or violence against Jews in order to avoid providing foreign propaganda with material against the Winter Olympics. Editors were asked not to refer to Rudi Ball as a Jew. This campaign succeeded beautifully and foreigners who attended the Winter Games came away suitably impressed. A piece appeared in the *New York Times* to the effect that there had been nothing military about the Games – and that those who reported otherwise were inaccurate. Foreign correspondents based in Germany on a more permanent basis resented this greatly, especially Westbrook Pegler who had virulently attacked the Nazis.

It would be wrong to think, however, that persecution of the Jews in Germany was completely discon-

tinued during the early months of 1936; it merely went on beneath the surface in a more subtle form. Although no new laws were passed and even the *Jewish Chronicle* could find no examples of personal violence against individuals, court actions for 'racial disgrace' still multiplied daily and secret police activity increased. No official pronouncements discriminated against Jewish businessmen, but somehow Jewish firms could not manage to get the supplies they needed and found themselves being advised on the quiet to sell out to Aryans. Jewish doctors could not practice in Aryan hospitals and Aryan doctors would not attend Jewish patients without permission from their local party office. Although the 'Olympic Way' between Munich and Garmisch had been purged of anti-Semitic signs, the roads from

Munich to Augsberg and Munich to Nuremberg still bristled with 'Swat the Jew' posters and the correspondent of the London *Daily Telegraph* reported that special care had to be taken during the Winter Games to protect Spanish athletes from 'unpleasantness' due to their non-Nordic features.

The job of polishing Germany's image went on after the Winter Games. In June editors were requested to 'use the Olympic Games and the preparations for them for extensive propaganda in Germany' and Goebbels was quoted as saying that 'the Olympic Games must and will be used to carry on propaganda for the New Germany

Above and right : **1935. The Berlin Olympic Stadium takes shape**

of Adolf Hitler. The propaganda will be chiefly on the lines of culture.' In order to advance the cause of culture a great national exhibition, 'Germany', was scheduled in Berlin from 18th July to 16th August. The lengthy sales pitch published by the GOC made no mention of its Nazi character; however, when the project was first made public on 13th October 1935 it was described as 'a concrete demonstration of National Socialist principles and programs' and the organizers stated that 'only things characteristic and typical will be

The Olympic Stadium (and the swimming pool on the left) nears completion

shown'. The Berlin Foreign Tourist Association acquired fleets of buses to provide visitors with free transport to labor camps and other National Socialist showplaces, and courteous 'contact men' called on certain tourists (chosen by their professions as listed in hotel registers) in order to ensure that they had a pleasant and instructive stay.

A *New York Times* correspondent observed in April that 'The visitor to Germany this summer who wants to avoid becoming Dr Goebbels' unconscious tool will have to possess an unusual amount of sales resistance and far more than the usual amount of modesty regarding the adequacy of his own hastily gained and carefully provided impressions.' The Propaganda Ministry stole a leaf from Intourist's book and prepared five conducted tours for Olympic visitors, paying special attention to the new party buildings in Munich and Nuremburg and to Hitler's new roads. Training of guides began and a register was established of automobile drivers, nursemaids and the like. In June Jewish paintings in the Berlin National Gallery were temporarily rehung and in July *The Times* of London reported that posters which showed the border of Germany encom-

KUNSTEISSTADION
H-PARTENKIRCHEN

ORGANISATIONSKOMITEE FÜR DIE
OLYMPISCHEN WINTERSPIELE 1936

BAULEITUNG:
ARCHITEKT D.W.B. HANNS OSTLER GARMISCH
UND DR. ING. E.H. RICHARD PAPST BERLIN

passing the Sudetenland had been confiscated.

Berlin was getting ready too; polishing and painting went on all over town and old buildings had a facelift. By March it was obvious that accommodation in the city was going to be a major problem, for in addition to the thousands of athletes and foreign visitors expected, the Strength Through Joy movement was planning to send as many of its members as possible to Berlin even though they had no hope of getting to see any of the events; 200,000 Germans had booked hotel rooms in Berlin for at least one night during the Games. At

Garmisch-Partenkirchen, site of the Winter Olympics scheduled for February 1936

first the organisers had planned to billet visitors only in the more modern sections of town; now a campaign was started to find rooms anywhere, regardless of their distance from the Stadium or the character of the neighborhood. The GOC also considered a plan to erect large television tents throughout Berlin to give people who could not get in some idea of what was going on.

In May the Minister of Finance released currency to buy food, for

Dr Rust, the Reich Minister of Education. In a clearly anti-Jewish warning he said that one of the qualifications necessary to train as an athletic instructor would be the applicant's ability as a political instructor

supplies for the Olympic Village had to be organized, and as early as June it was almost impossible to buy an egg in the city. Another item on the organizers' shopping list was 50,000 grapefruits, and the *Daily Telegraph* observed sardonically that the Minister had put off releasing the money for food until the grapefruit season in Palestine was over. (Palestine, it may be noted, was one of the few countries with Olympic organizations to decline Germany's invitation to the Games.) Another item that elicited caustic comments from the world press was the announcement that only German press photographers would be present at the Games and that the Olympic Motion Picture Company would have sole filming rights. 'Clearly', said the *New York Times*, 'the world is to see the Olympic Games through German lenses, and no opportunity for political propaganda will be ignored.'

In another attempt to placate the IOC an official order issued in April stated that it was now illegal to expel Jews from sports groups, pointing out that Paragraph Four of the Constitution of the Reich Association of Physical Culture (which barred Jews from membership) had become invalid on 1st January 1936. It had little effect on the actual presence of Jews on the Olympic team since most of them had been thrown out long before 1st January. The order also granted the Association the right to 'reject any application for membership if it does not think the applicant fit, but it must not base the rejection on the lack of Aryan qualifications.' A note to the order stated that this procedure involved no difficulties since 'it is neither necessary nor expedient to

quote grounds'. There were other indications of the position of Jews in the German sporting world. Dr Rust, the Minister of Education, in his opening speech at the new Reich Academy of Athletics, said that a strict selection of candidates for the honor of being trained as athletic and sports instructors would be necessary and that in Berlin one of the qualifications would be the applicant's ability as a political instructor. This was a strange statement coming from one who shortly before had been bemoaning the tendency of protestors to bring politics into sport, and was also a clear warning that no Jews need apply. At the end of July newspapers in Germany were ordered not to report about Jewish members of foreign teams or to comment at all about Jews in the Olympic Games.

One final example will suffice to show Germany's attitude to the Games at this time, in the form of a message from *Reichssportsführer* von Tschammer und Osten to all Germans throughout the world who would be coming to the Olympic Games in Berlin. It was originally published in the magazine *Der Deutsche im Ausland* and said in part, 'hospitable Germany welcomes this opportunity of answering the flood of propaganda that has spread through the world with actual examples, and of revealing to hundreds of thousands of visitors the true conditions which prevail . . . Every German heart will beat faster and every eye will shine for joy at the opportunity of meeting and talking with countrymen from the outer world. The Germany which welcomes them is again a powerful nation which will be represented at the Olympic Games by a proud and unified sporting organization. . . The thousands of Germans from abroad will find on their arrival a Germany that not only enters the combat joyously but also emerges victorious, and a country that will stand behind them in their own tasks.'

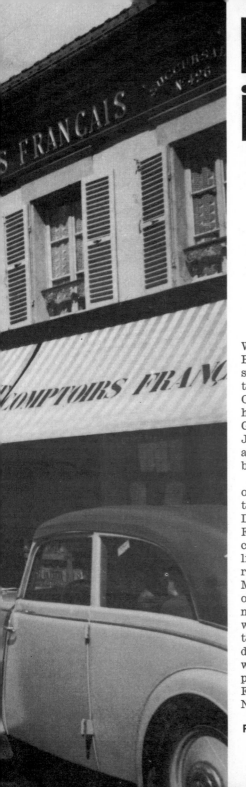

Politics in sport

With fifty-three nations entered in the Berlin Games and over 5,000 athletes scheduled to compete, international tensions were bound to affect the Olympic Games. International Jewry had long been crying out against Nazi Germany, and in countries with large Jewish populations the battle waged against the Games was especially bitter.

But in France the fight was mainly on political grounds. As early as 1933 the Vice-President of the Chamber of Deputies, M Pate, was urging the French Olympic Committee to boycott the 1936 Games. But there was little popular opposition until Hitler re-militarized the Rhineland on 7th March 1936. Two days later a French official declared that Germany's renunciation of the Locarno Pact would probably mean the collapse of the Olympic Games, and that France definitely would not attend; the next week the French government postponed allocating a subsidy for the French team pending League of Nations action against Germany.

Propaganda for the Games in France

Louis Rimet, President of the French National Sports Committee. One of the leading spokesmen in calling on France to boycott the Games, he said that 'One is a Frenchman before one is an Olympic competitor'

Leading French sportsmen were prominent figures at the protest meetings held during March and April by the International Committee for the Preservation of the Olympic Spirit, Friends of Sport and other interested bodies. Dr Bellin du Coteau, President of the International Hockey League, Bernard Levy, President of the Racing Club of Paris, M Drigny, President of the International Swimming Association and M Jacob, Vice-President of the Paris League of Athletics, joined other liberals and sportsmen in calling on France to boycott the Games and not give Germany money for propaganda purposes. 'One is a Frenchman before one is an Olympic competitor', said Louis Rimet, President of the French National Sports Committee.

The final decision on participation was left to Leon Blum's Popular Front government which came to power in May. On 6th and 7th June the International Fair Play Committee held a conference in Paris and adopted a four-point resolution: 1. Urging that delegates be sent to Germany to investigate the extent of Nazi control of sports and government interference with the Olympic Games. 2. Applauding the news that Great Britain was to send a team to the 'Peoples Olympics' in Barcelona in July. 3. Calling for a letter to be sent to the International Olympic Committee asking if, by supporting the Berlin Olympics, it supported Nazism. 4. Agreeing that all university athletes had a standing invitation to the Barcelona Games and approving of a protest rally in Trafalgar Square organized by the British Fair Play Committee. In the end, however, after much debate the government finally approved the original grant and a French team was sent to Berlin.

Great Britain received her invitation to compete in the Games towards the end of 1933, but put off accepting it until December 1934. Twelve months later the decision was reviewed and, after 'careful consideration of all the facts', was reaffirmed. The British Olympic Association then decided to make an appeal for funds to send the British team to Germany, and to embody in the appeals letter the full reasons which prompted the acceptance of Germany's invitation. That appeals letter stated the arguments in favor of acceptance so clearly that a good part of it is worthy of reproduction: 'The British Olympic Committee are convinced that in sending a team to Berlin they are acting in the best interests of sport. The Olympic Games have always stood for the ideal of harmony and reconciliation between nations, and it would be nothing short of calamity if, at this very critical stage in world affairs, this country, to whom the world so often looks for a lead, were not fully represented at (this) gathering. Great Britain's team will be chosen without any regard whatsoever to the origin, religious belief or political creed of the competitors. The

Léon Blum, French Prime Minister. A socialist and a Jew, he delayed giving government finance to the French Olympic Committee until the very last minute

Neville Chamberlain, British Chancellor of the Exchequer. The British government's attitude to the Games was ambivalent, but in the end it decided against mixing sport with politics and refused to boycott

team which we shall send to Germany will be a united one representing the British people, and no Briton of whatever origin or persuasion need have any hesitation in approving the support given by the BOC to the Games. The Council have the full assurance of those responsible for organizing the Games that there will be no demonstrations or discriminations against any competitors.

'We appeal to your generosity and patriotism to help us to maintain not only Great Britain's reputation in games and sportsmanship, but the influential place the country has always occupied in the world's affairs.'

Many congresses and rallies were also held during January in connection with the Games, and invitations to participate therein were forwarded to all the country's amateur athletic bodies. In Great Britain, therefore, fewer of the leaders in the sports world supported the protest movement than in France, but joined with Sir Noel Curtis Bennett in deploring

attempts to mix sport with politics.

Early in January 1936 the National Workers' Sports Association tried to organize a special General Meeting of the Amateur Athletic Association in order to call for a boycott of the Games; although several athletic clubs scattered throughout the country joined them in their plea, including the London Labour Sports Association which had 3,000 members, the NWSA failed to gain the support of enough clubs to constitute a quorum. Throughout January and February news stories about the banning of Jewish athletes in Germany and quotations from the more rabid Jew-baiters ('We can see no possible value for our people in permitting dirty Jews and Negroes to travel through our country and compete in athletics with our best') were circulated in the press, and the *Manchester Guardian* came out strongly in favor of a boycott, asking 'Who thrust politics into sport in the first

place?' In London the NWSA produced an exhibition of Workers' Sport, with contributions from France, Belgium, the United States, Holland, Switzerland, Finland, Norway and Czechoslovakia, and a lecture by the Chairman, George Elvin, on the reasons behind the protest. At Oxford University *Isis*, an influencial students' magazine, came out against the Berlin Olympics.

The Annual Meeting of the Amateur Athletic Association was scheduled for 21st March and the NWSA had their motion ready well in advance. 'This Annual Meeting of the AAA,' it stated, 'is of the opinion that the spirit which is promoted by the organisation of the Olympic Games cannot be forwarded by participation in the 1936 Olympic Games and instructs the Association to withdraw its support and withhold the necessary permission to any of its members who may make an application to compete.' The motion was withdrawn, however, after the meeting opened since Elvin could not manage to get enough support for it. It was decided to reconvene the meeting in two months' time to consider the proposition. This was as much as the protesters had hoped for and they left considering that they had scored a great success.

By this time the furor over Britain's participation was so great that the question was debated in the House of Commons. Cdr Locker-Lampson, a Conservative Member of Parliament, asked Neville Chamberlain, then Chancellor of the Exchequer, whether he was aware that the Olympic Games would assist Germany to the extent of several million pounds which was being used for armaments, and suggested that the Chancellor consider prohibiting British money to be used for this

A Berlin park sign. The top one asks citizens to keep their dogs on the lead ; the bottom one says that the yellow benches are for the use of Jews. Hitler ordered the removal of similar anti-Jewish signs

purpose. W S Morrison, answering for the government, replied that they had no power to prevent people spending money in Germany. Mrs Ellen Wilkinson, later to become Minister of Education, commented that if the Germans ran the Olympic Games the way they had run their recent elections, there would be one only competitor in each event. Later, on 13th July, Locker-Lampson raised the matter again, asking the Secretary of State for Foreign Affairs whether, in view of the announcement that minorities were to be treated well in Germany until after the Olympic Games in August when, presumably, the persecution would be resumed, he would arrange to withhold passport facilities from persons who wished to visit Germany. But the Viscount Cranbourne replied 'I have no knowledge of any such announcement as that referred to by my honourable and gallant friend.' Later that same month the boycott faction tried again: Mr Eden was asked whether he would ask the German government for an assurance that the Olympic Games would not be used for propaganda purposes. Mr Eden's reply was short and to the point. 'No, sir' he said.

The National Workers' Sports Association – now renamed the British Workers' Sports Association – continued their agitation through April and finally, at their Annual General Meeting, decided to call for a special meeting of the Amateur Athletic Association as had been agreed in March. This was duly convened on 23rd May when, though the BWSA confidently expected more support than at the previous meeting, their motion was thrown out by an overwhelming majority. Oddly enough, it was a speech by a noted Jewish athlete, Mr H L Abrahams, at the meeting in March that was thought to have swung the balance in favor of participation. Another factor may have been the wide publicity given to those favoring participation during the month of May.

The British Olympic Association held its annual dinner on the 19th in an atmosphere of comaraderie and mutual good will. Dr Lewald, the guest of honor, presented Hitler as a 'firm believer in the peace-creating influence of sport', and Sir Thomas Inskip, Minister of Coordination of Defence, expressed the hope that one result of Berlin would be to make his job a sinecure. Sir Thomas sat next to Prince Otto von Bismarck during dinner and, as he told reporters afterwards, they decided that if it was left to them to settle international affairs in the spirit of the banquet, they could do so very quickly. 'Germany can count on many warm hearts in this country', Inskip affirmed.

In the May issue of *World Sport* an article by a 'Well-Known British Sportsman' bemoaned the fact that 'an evil miasma has recently clouded the sportsman's horizons' and went on to beg his readers 'not in any way to mix politics with sport. They make poor companions, and if other countries have government-controlled sport, that is no concern of ours.' That same issue carried an article by Lord Aberdare who asserted that 'Hitler has not tried to influence or control the Games in any way. His only concern is that Germany's guests shall be happy and come away satisfied.' He went on to give a most convincing account of the history of the allocation of the Games, mentioning the GOC's guarantee in 1932 that they were independent of the government and that Jews would not be excluded from German teams. He noted that this pledge had been reaffirmed at his (Aberdare's) request in 1934, the GOC producing letters from Jewish sports organisations to prove that Jewish athletes had an even better opportunity to participate in the 1936 Olympics than they had ever had before. An investigation of claims of discrimination had revealed them to have no basis in fact; it should be remembered that there was only one Jew on the German team in 1932 and

A London shop window

that the number of Jews on the British team was infinitesimal.

In London *The Times*, perhaps the most influential newspaper in Britain, struck a generally doleful note about German affairs throughout 1936, though it did not actually come out in favor of a boycott. In January it reported the relaxation of anti-Jewish activity, and expressed the opinion that this was only a temporary whitewash. This opinion was repeated in July, though the news columns carried a wide range of comment, from the report of the Special Correspondent who said 'Incidents are only incidents' and extolled the surge of Olympic feeling in Germany; to that of *The Times*' Berlin correspondent who saw the Olympic Games as a purely internal political event having nothing whatsoever to do with the Olympic spirit. The debate went on in the letters column as well, with the pro-participation party getting a

slight edge. One correspondent suggested that the next Olympic Games be held in the only place he could think of where there was no suppressed minority, where no national pride would be shown in the organization of the Games and no profit made on them, and where there was a 100% divorce between athletics and military efficiency – the South Seas.

All over Europe demonstrations were organized, athletes refused their invitations and governments talked (but on the whole did no more than talk) about boycotting the Games. In 1933 one hundred sportsmen in Yugoslavia issued a manifesto against the Games and a letter from the Committee for the Preservation of the Olympic Ideal gained wide publicity. In 1934 demonstrations in Sweden against a visit by a German football team managed to reduce attendance at their games to less than 2,000. Meetings were held in Prague in January and February of 1936 and the Executive Council of the Czech Football

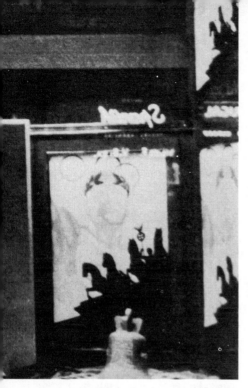

fused to compete. Austria did not look kindly toward the Games and in Vienna thirty of the forty-three chess clubs called on their Federation to abstain from the Chess Olympiad held in Munich in August. Spain decided at the last minute to send a team to Berlin, then had to withdraw it again because of the Civil War. The Belgian Football Association and the Saint Gallen (a Swiss swimming organization) refused to take part, and many European athletes refused individually to attend. Several South American countries did not send teams to Berlin; perhaps in an effort to make up for this Brazil sent two – but since no one could decide which was the official team, both had to withdraw. Some athletes who did not want to go to Berlin, like the Polish boxer Rotholz, found themselves expelled from their sports clubs for their position, and one Jew who happened to be in the army was forced to participate.

Generally speaking the movement against the Games was led by the trade unions and by Jewish organizations. The biggest battle of all raged in the United States where there were not only a good number of Jews on the Olympic team, but where Jews were very active in athletic associations and contributed liberally to the Olympic fund. Compared to the discussion in Great Britain, which on the whole was conducted along gentlemanly lines, the American situation resembled nothing so much as a dog fight.

In 1933 the American Olympic Committee met in Washington and a special sub-committee passed a resolution which, while pledging support to the International Olympic Committee and the German Organizing Committee, expressed the hope that all disabilities affecting the rights of Jewish athletes to train, compete for and be on German teams would be removed. Later that year, in November, a Convention of the AOC passed yet another resolution protesting discrimination in Germany and asking

Association decided not to send a team to the Olympics. In February the Czech Minister of Finance threatened to withold a government grant, but even in March the government was stalling, waiting to see further political developments.

There were mass meetings in Toronto, and Dutch athletes held a meeting in Amsterdam. This last meeting was attended by two Dutch marathon champions and the President of the Dutch Catholic Football Association, and received a telegram of congratulations from one of the members of the Netherlands Olympic Committee. There was a great deal of opposition to the Games in Holland, and in May an exhibition was planned in Amsterdam to take place during the Games to 'expose the Nazi concepts of culture'. In Sweden, too, there was a lot of opposition, led by the trade unions. Since most Swedish athletes were trade union members there was some fear that she could not send a team at all, and in fact several top athletes re-

Avery Brundage. In 1933 he reported to the American Olympic Committee that after comprehensive and searching enquiries he was satisfied that Jewish athletes in Germany were not being discriminated against. On the strength of his report the American Committee accepted Germany's invitation

that restrictions on Jewish athletes be removed by 1936 so that American athletes could participate. Germany promised in reply that no restrictions would be placed on Jews; but the Committee was still not satisfied and when their invitation was received early in 1934 the decision whether to accept or reject it was referred to an executive committee pending Avery Brundage's fact-finding visit to Germany. Mr Brundage, a member of the IOC Executive Committee, made his trip in September and returned to report that after comprehensive and searching enquiries he was satisfied that Jewish athletes in Germany were not being discriminated against. On the strength of this remarkable report the AOC decided to accept Germany's invitation; although the American Jewish Congress immediately contacted the Amateur Athletic Union and asked them to review the decision,

that action was postponed until 1935.

In July 1935 the real battle began. Mr Jeremiah T Mahoney, a former New York State Supreme Court Justice and a leader in the Amateur Athletic Union, announced that he would vote against United States participation if the reports he had been hearing about discrimination in Germany were confirmed. During August the number of people opposing the Games grew and discussions even took place in Congress. In the Senate Peter G Gerry (Rhode Island) and David I Walsh (Massachusetts) asked that the United States consider withdrawing from the Games, and in the House of Representatives Emanual Celler (New York) proposed discouraging the use of public funds to finance the trip. In September Governor Earle of Pennyslvania was demanding United States withdrawal, the National Council of Methodist Youth prepared a boycott petition and at its convention in Atlantic City the AFL passed a resolution condemning participation. In October Mahoney produced a long list of German violations of the Olympic rules and the ranks of the protestors grew to include George Shuster, the editor of Commonweal; William Green, President of the AFL; the mayor of New York City, Fiorello La Guardia; the President of Holyoke College and many other influential Americans, including even Father Coughlin in Detroit, the notorious anti-semitic priest.

Just a few days before the National Convention of the AAU in December a mass meeting was held in New York City to whip up support; Walter White of the NAACP joined Governor Earle, Mayor La Guardia, Mr Mahoney and other prominent figures in urging the AAU to withdraw its members from the competition. The convention itself was a stormy one, with Mahoney refusing to stand for the Presidency and Brundage being elected over the issue of the Berlin Olympics. When a vote was taken, those in favor of participation won by the narrowest

Fiorello La Guardia, Mayor of New York City. In October 1935 he joined the powerful American movement protesting against German violations of the Olympic rules

of margins (sixty-one to fifty-five) and the officers who had been against it walked out, led by Mahoney. 'The United States will go to the Olympics no matter what', was Brundage's reaction.

The American Goodwill Athletic Union to Preserve the Olympic Ideal was officially incorporated on 4th January 1936, organized by Samuel K Maccabee who was also the Chairman of the Move the Olympics Committee. They disseminated anti-German propaganda and eventually won many people over to their point of view.

The League of American Writers was one organisation that opposed the Games. One of their members, W L Phelps, participated on a committee to select American literature on sport to be compared with that of other nations at the Olympic Games; the League sent him an open letter expressing their shock that 'an enlightened person . . . should lend himself to the forces of reaction and barbarism'. Three colleges refused to

play in the Olympic basketball trials: Long Island University plainly stated that they would not under any circumstances be represented at any Olympic Games held in Germany; at New York University the decision was left to the players, and the team – which was mainly Jewish – decided that they could not spare the time from their studies; Notre Dame simply issued a statement to the effect that they could not participate since the tryouts would require the players to be away from classes too long.

In April the American Olympic Committee hit the headlines again when they expelled one of their members, Mr Charles L Ornstein, for failure to cooperate with the Committee. The occasion marked Ornstein's first appearance at a Committee meeting since the AAU convention in December; he had not resigned like all the other opponents of the Games. He had come to protest the high-handed tactics of Roy Davis, Chairman of the Chicago Boxing Commission, but before he could mention the subject a motion was put forward to remove him from the committee, since he had missed two consecutive meetings and had not answered an AOC questionnaire about willingness to cooperate over the Berlin Olympics. Ornstein protested that he had had a good reason for missing one meeting and had not been notified of the second. The meeting was generally calm, though there were several sharp exchanges between Ornstein and Avery Brundage, and the Treasurer, Gustavus T Kirby expressed the opinion at one point that anyone who hadn't the decency to resign ought to be made to do so. Finally Ornstein asked to be given until the next meeting to think the whole matter over, but this was denied and he was voted off the Committee with only one dissention. He was, understandably, very bitter about this and next day issued a virulent statement to the press complaining that the AOC had 'adopted

the color and tactics of Nazi Germany' and that their 'illegal' action had been dictated by the fear that the Olympic question would be reopened and the American team withdrawn.

Money, as usual, was another problem. The AOC could not expect any support from Jews or their liberal supporters. Avery Brundage issued a statement at the end of April complaining that, although the prospects looked good and his fundraisers were enthusiastic, he could get no idea of how much money the AOC actually had or was likely to receive. In May the Massachusetts State Legislature rejected a bill to donate $10,000 towards the United States team's expenses – another victory for the anti-Olympics movement.

Many influential newspapers supported the boycott, and the *New York Times* was one of the most active. Their opposition took the form mainly of pointing out discrepancies between Germany's actions, especially regarding her Jewish population, and her professed belief in the Olympic ideals of fair play. In March the editor noted that anti-Jewish posters were

Above and right : **Streicher and Goebbels, the leading German Jew baiters**

being removed in Berlin and wondered if the way to secure decent treatment for non-Aryans in Germany was to hold the Olympic Games there every year. Perhaps, he thought, after practicing decent self-control for a couple of weeks each winter and a month or two in summer the habit would spread through the rest of Germany and the rest of the year.

In April the *Reich Sport Journal*, a weekly magazine, began to be circulated world-wide. Its content was about one-half sports news and one-half political propaganda, and it referred often to the theory that sport was essentially a political function, as training for service in the National Socialist sense. The April issue contained a picture of Hitler reviewing a group of enthusiastically saluting athletes captioned 'Only one will must lead us. We must build a whole, and the same discipline binds us together in obedience and subordination to order, and do not forget, it is for our

country,' This, said *The Times*, 'was a brave attempt to scramble the ideal of Olympic open competition and the Nazi goosestep. Perhaps when the two had become assimilated we would not be treated to such outrageous displays of unbridled individuality as had marred earlier Olympic contests'. The One Will would decide who ran fastest, jumped highest, etc. And when *Olympic Games 1936* quoted Hitler as saying that 'An honorable and fair struggle awakens the best in man' *The Times* wondered if one could call the struggle of 66,550,000 Germans against 450,000 of their fellow citizens 'fair and honorable' and if so, if that struggle brought out the best in Julius Streicher and Joseph Goebbels.

The outcome of the controversy we all know; despite the opposition and despite various incidents involving the team members at the Games, the United States team – with its customary contingent of Jews and Negroes – not only swept through the Games in more than adequate fashion but managed to give Hitler's Aryan superiority theories a black eye in the process. Avery Brundage noted rather bitterly in his report after the Games that 'Every sort of social, political and economic pressure was exerted against the officials and members of the AOC and all kinds of obstacles placed in their way . . . the country was flooded with misleading propaganda until many people who should have known better were influenced.' It must be remembered that, despite all the rhetoric bandied about at the time, the AAU and AOC officials who were in favor of participation were probably no more in sympathy with Hitler's anti-Jewish policies than were the men who were opposed to it. They were only, as Brundage puts it, 'Clinging steadfastly to the principle that sport must be kept free from politics' – insisting that the competition would be in the hands of the IOC, that Hitler would have nothing to do with it other than making an opening and closing address, that the United States would be competing under the Olympic not the Swastika flag, and that their presence could not possibly be considered an endorsement of Hitler's racial policies.

The 'Rival' Olympic Games

One of the results of the movement opposing the Olympic Games was a series of 'rival' Olympics held by various groups. The Jewish Olympics were held in Tel Aviv in 1935. A Prague Olympiad was planned, as was a Workers' Olympiad scheduled for Antwerp in 1937.

One program which attracted the attention of many sportsmen was the ill-fated Peoples' Olympiad which was planned for 19th–26th July in Barcelona. With active support from the international trade union movement as well as the Comintern, prospects for the Peoples' Olympiad looked rosy by the beginning of June. Sportsmen from Europe and America were completing their plans to attend as a 'final gesture of protest against the Hitler Nazi Games in Berlin', they would have free room and board in Spain, but would have to pay their own fares – the national athletic associations, with a few exceptions, would not provide any funds. In England the Amateur Athletic Association tried to stop English athletes competing on the grounds that the Spanish AAA did not recognize the

Spanish Republican troops in Barcelona where one of the 'rival' Olympic Games, the People's Olympiad, became involved in the Spanish civil war before it got off the ground

45

Peoples' Olympiad. But the British Workers' Sports Association sent a telegram to the Spanish organization and received a reply stating that not only were they perfectly willing to recognize the Peoples' Games, but that they had informed the English AAA of this fact some six weeks previously. The AAA withdrew their ban. By contrast, the French government took a highly sympathetic view and issued a grant of 600,000 francs to her 1,200-member Peoples' Olympiad team (as opposed to a 1,000,000-franc grant to the team attending the Berlin Olympics).

On 4th July the nine Americans who had decided to compete in Barcelona set sail on the SS *Transylvania*, sponsored by the Committee for Fair Play in Sports. Forty-one British athletes left London on the 17th, led by George Elvin and accompanied by four Scots pipers. By the 18th all the athletes were gathered together in a Barcelona gay with big brilliantly-colored posters. The next day at four in the afternoon Senor Luis Companys, President of the Generalidad (Prime Minister of Catalonia) opened the Games which were to include not only the regular Olympic events, but folk singing, dancing and theatricals, as well as an 800-board chess tournament. 'This is not an event for any political party nor an assembly of stars', he stated. 'The Peoples' Olympiad will revive the original spirit of the Olympic Games – the games intended for the people.'

Alas, the people were not going to get their games – at least not that summer in Spain. The opening ceremonies were held, but on Sunday morning troops, who had been awakened early, given a generous ration of brandy and set out to march around the city with clenched fists (the Communist salute) ostensibly to celebrate the opening of the games, attacked the government under the leadership of Colonel Lopez Amor. Crowds of people stood in tense silence throughout the city listening to the radio news bulletins as the noise of rifle and machine gun fire grew louder and louder; games were the furthest thing from their minds. Several days of confusion followed as no one knew what was happening to the games or to the athletes who were to participate in them.

Finally, on 22nd July, a report reached the *Daily Worker* in London: 'The British team . . . is having a novel but interesting time in Barcelona. After the opening ceremonies the commencement of the actual sports events have been delayed due to the conditions caused by the Fascist attempt at rebellion. The British and all foreign athletes are accomodated at a palatial hotel in Barcelona.' Many athletes left quite soon for Marsailles, full of plans to carry on the games in Paris, but many others stayed on; the ranks of the Thaelmann Centuria and the Gastone-Sozzi Battalion of the International Brigade were swelled by part of the German and Italian teams who had come to Spain via Russia after exiling themselves from their own countries. The *New York Times* reported that the United States athletes were cheering on the Catalonian government in its fight against the rebels; 'Everything OK notify parents situation well in hand don't worry' was a typical telegram sent back home. The United States team finally set sail for New York, having taken more than a passive part in the revolution. They had, they said, been shot at, obliged to loot for food and guns, helped to build barricades and had been called in as advisors to the Barcelona government. They made no mention of a palatial hotel.

Sportsmen who stayed in the United States had a less exciting time of it politically, but at least they did manage to complete their competitions. The World Labor Athletic Carnival was conceived and organized by the leaders of the unsuccessful boycott movement; Charles Ornstein announced plans for the carnival in

Mrs Ellen Wilkinson, British MP. She commented that if the Germans ran the Olympic Games the way they had run their recent elections, there would only be one competitor in each event

May 1936, ably supported by J T Mahoney, Ralph Manning, President of the United States Football Federation, and Dan Ferris, Secretary-Treasurer of the Amateur Athletic Union who was acting in an advisory capacity on the assurance that there would be no interference with the Olympic Games.

Nor was there any overt interference with Berlin, despite the fact that the organizers and supporters of the event had generally opposed that meet. The avowed purpose of the World Labor Athletic Carnival was to 'stimulate amateur athletics as a profitable means of utilizing the amount of leisure now enjoyed by workers', and there is no record of any athlete who made the Olympic team in the tryouts turning it down in favor of the Athletic Carnival. Nevertheless, the affair received more publicity and support than it would ordinarily have done and many more athletes who were not trade unionists participated because of its anti-Olympic connotations.

The meet was scheduled to be held on 15th and 16th August, coinciding with the last two days of the Olympics; an impressive entry list, carefully marshalled by Abel Kiviat and Charles Ornstein from fifteen states, Canada, thirty clubs and twenty-two colleges, included a large representation of record holders, both great and small. Among the contestants George Varoff from San Francisco was the world's record holder in the pole vault; Tom Ottey was the champion steeplechaser at the 1932 Los Angeles Olympics; and Charley Beetham of Ohio State held the United States championship in the 800-metre event. Seven of the trackmen were well within the 09.8–09.5 second range for the 100-yard dash: Eddie Daigle of Loyola New Orleans, Perrin Walker from Georgia, ex-navy star John Waybright, former national champions Eulace Peacock and Ben Johnson, Ed O'Sullivan of the New York Curb Exchange and Philadelphia ace Joe Hall. The presence of all these fine athletes guaranteed some exciting performances; many would be going through their paces with a thoughtful eye on Berlin, spurred on by their failure to make the Olympic team. More than 500 athletes were scheduled to compete, and advance ticket sales netted $35,000; Governor Herbert Lehman put up a trophy and Mayor La Guardia provided a cup for the leading labor union team.

On Saturday, 15th August some 7,500 hardy fans were on hand at the stadium on Randalls Island, New York, for opening day. An early threat of rain had cut attendance and no records were broken that day, but it made no difference to the small but enthusiastic crowd who rocked the stadium with their cheers.

A roar went up during the second semi-final of the 100-metre sprint when Eustace Peacock, three-time winner over Jesse Owens, suffered a recurrence of the leg injury that had kept him out of the Olympic trials. The long-striding Temple University

Negro, who was heavily favored to win, had previously breezed to victory in his heat. In the semi-final he was second to Perrin Walker and coming on strong when he suddenly pulled up lame. It is a tribute to his great ability that he still managed to finish third in spite of his handicap.

In the final, Perrin Walker showed his heels to a strong field. Bob Rodenkirchen, the schoolboy prodigy from Jersey City, jumped into the lead, with Ed O'Sullivan close behind. Then about half way along the powerfully built senior from Georgia Tech put on a burst of speed and began moving up from fourth place. He swept past Phil Cody and then there was no stopping him; flying high, wide and handsome he took the others in his stride and triumphed easily over O'Sullivan in second place, Cody in third and Rodenkirchen, who had faded back into fourth.

The mile run was just as exciting, with Ernst Federoff of Millhouse AA sprinting desperately up from nowhere out of a pack of twenty-two to beat Patrick White of Jamaica Long Island by six yards. Gilder Farrow won almost as he pleased in the 220-yard low hurdle and Walter Stone of Michigan captured the two-mile steeplechase with even less trouble. Pete Zaremba of the New York Athletic Club tossed the 56lb weight 34 feet 1½ inches for a win and Roy Allee annexed the 16lb shot-put with a heave of 49 feet 5½ inches. The javelin throw was captured by a schoolboy from Oklahoma City, Bob Peoples, with an effort of 198 feet 1¾ inches and Lou Gregory of Millhouse AA won the grueling five-mile run.

Next day the weather improved and Governor Lehman, falling into the spirit of the occasion, picked out a comfortable seat on the grass, doffed his straw hat, and with as much enthusiasm and anxiety as anyone else trained his eyes on the cross bar above his head. It was the tensest moment of the two-day meet; pole

vault star George Varoff, the San Francisco janitor who had missed the boat to Berlin, had just cleared 14 feet 4½ inches, surpassing Earl Meadow's winning height in the Olympics with plenty to spare. Now he was priming himself to better his own world's mark of 14 feet 6½ inches. The bar was raised to 14 feet 7 inches and a hush fell over the crowd as the national champion stormed down the runway with muscles straining, threw himself upwards and sailed over, only to knock the bar down with his feet as he descended. On his second try he got completely over, but somehow his wrist got in the way and down came the bar again. Disheartened, he never even came close on his third and final attempt, but even before the bar had fallen into the pit a tumultuous ovation rocked the stadium. For his brilliant work the blond Pacific Coast athlete was awarded the Senator Benjamin F Berman Trophy.

It was a busy afternoon for the Governor as, in addition to watching the pole vaulting exhibition, he started one of the closed events (for labor union members only) and kicked out the ball to launch a soccer game between the New York Americans and Ulster United of Toronto, as well as presenting the trophy he had donated to Millhouse AA as the team scoring the most points.

There were other performers beside Varoff who won the plaudits of the crowd that day. Walker breezed from behind again to beat Bob Rodenkirchen in the 220-yard dash in 20.8 seconds, and long distance ace Lou Gregory added the three-mile test to his five-mile victory, while burly Pete Zaremba topped his 56lb weight throw of the day before with a winning 16lb hammer toss. The World Labor Athletic Carnival at Randall's Island had been a huge success and the organizers happily began planning for an indoor winter meet at Madison Square Garden, and for annual summer events thereafter.

Aside from this one fine athletic

Indem ich mich des Juden erwehre
kämpfe ich für das Werk des Herrn

'By resisting the Jew, I fight for the Lord' –
a placard on the SA Headquarters in
Nuremberg, 1935

event, the opposition movement had no direct effect. Despite all their work, the innumerable committees that had been formed had not managed to disrupt the Berlin Games or to have them moved; despite all their threats, no country of any importance finally boycotted the competition. But it can be argued that the glare of publicity directed upon Germany by her enemies forced her to soften her attitude towards her Jewish population, at least temporarily. In fact,

one of the things that made the Games such a success with visitors was this downgrading of some of the more unpleasant aspects of Nazism; perhaps by helping to make this downgrading necessary, the opposition movement actually contributed to the *success* of the XI Olympics.

Winter Olympics

On 2nd February 1936, in a blinding snowstorm, Adolf Hitler officially opened the IV Winter Olympics before a capacity crowd of 15,000. Between the 2nd and the 16th the eyes of the world were on Garmisch-Partenkirchen, as people waited to see not only the results of the sports contest, but whether the dire predictions of the opponents of the Berlin Olympics would come true. In a sense both sides found that the Games – which marked the first time both the summer and winter contests had been held in the same country – reinforced the opinions they had held previously; the pro-participation party found in the absence of overt anti-Semitism a justification of their position, while the opponents of participation saw this and the good publicity which resulted from it as further evidence of German hypocricy and the dangers of allowing the Summer Games to take place.

The main contingent of the United States team set off early in January, with a happy jolly crowd numbering

2nd February 1936. Hitler, Göring, Frau Göring and Goebbels at the Winter Olympics at Garmisch-Partenkirchen. This was the first time that both the summer and winter contests had been held in the same country

51

in the hundreds coming to see them
off as they set sail on the USS *Manhattan*. The weather, which had jinxed
the three previous Winter Olympics,
was warm and drizzly and it looked as
if the fourth would be seriously
threatened. Only five days before
they were due to begin the *New York
Times* reported that although the snow
at Garmisch was still satisfactory the
ice was getting soft and the bob-sled run
was useless. But at the last possible
minute the weather changed and
remained well-nigh perfect throughout. The bob-sled run was repaired and
the Games were able to proceed; as
soon as they were over, the warm
weather returned.

Even the *New York Times* could not
deny that on opening day Germany

**The teams parade in front of the
ski-jump slope. The weather which had
detracted from the three previous
Winter Olympics was warm and drizzly
and it looked as if the fourth would be
seriously threatened**

The German curling team marches past during the opening ceremonies. The question now remained, would the dire predictions of the opponents of the German Olympic Games come true?

was, as a host, near enough perfect and that better organization and facilities for information could not have been desired. The broadcasting arrangements which were to elict so much praise in August were put to the test: some 300 reports and commentaries were broadcast to nineteen countries during the ten days of the event. There were many instances of the famous German efficiency; for example, a huge restaurant and assembly hall, intended to cater for the 5,000 Strength Through Joy members in town for the Games, was begun and finished in the fortnight preceeding opening day. Profiteering was eliminated by setting fixed prices for everything before the influx of tourists

A loudspeaker goes up at Garmisch,
increasing further the visitors'
impressions that the Germans were
providing unrivaled facilities

arrived. Not the slightest sign of
religious, political or racial prejudice
was outwardly visible and it was
evident that Germany was determined
that only sports would count during
that ten-day period. William Shirer,
an American correspondent who had
come down from Berlin thought that
there were too many SS troops and
military about, but had to admit that
the scenery was superb, the mountain
air exhilarating, the girls attractive
and the games exciting – on the whole,
a wonderful propaganda job.

Of course, there had to be some
snags. Before the Games began the
American bob-sled team became involved in a bitter dispute with the
German organizers when they insisted
on using their own sleds for the race.
These sleds, which had given them a
great advantage in 1932, had sharper

runners than those used by European
teams and the Germans declared that
they would not be suitable in Garmisch because of the condition of the
snow. But the Americans invaded the
headquarters building, shouting and
screaming and threatening, and finally
the Germans backed down. Near the
end of the Games a fist-fight threatened to stop a match between the two
leading ice hockey teams, Great
Britain and Canada.

A procedural question confronting
the participants was that of deciding
how to salute during the march past the
reviewing stand on opening day. The
Olympic Salute consists of extending
the arm out to the side, and bears a
distinct resemblence to the salute
used by the Nazis, though it was
chosen long before that particular
manifestation came into fashion. The
British team, opting to use it on the

**The skating rink. The Americans, used
to indoor rinks, found the experience
of skating outside unsettling**

grounds that they wanted their salute to be seen and feeling that an 'eyes right' delivered by untrained men and women would not be noticed, were disconcerted to hear the broadcaster announce 'The British greet the German Führer with the German Salute!' The Americans chose 'eyes right' and as a further gesture did not follow custom and dip their flag as they passed the reviewing stand. Estonia and Finland were two other countries who declined to give the Olympic Salute.

Garmisch-Partenkirchen was well-known for its bob-sled run on which several international races had been held and on which several men had lost their lives. For the Games it was improved and heightened at the bends and made faster by the ingenious use of ice blocks sunk into the track. As bumps appeared the blocks could be taken out, and new ones put in and frozen over, by a special process; thus the track was out of commission only for a few minutes during practice and

The bob-sled run, before and during the Games. It was improved and heightened at the bends and made faster by the use of ice blocks sunk into the track – as bumps appeared the blocks could be taken out and new ones put in and frozen over

competition, which was a good thing since practice time had been badly curtailed by the weather.

The United States team was one of the finest ever assembled to engage in this dangerous sport; most of the men were tall, good-looking moun-taineers from the Adirondacks and were splendid athletes. They were among the competitors who went off to St Moritz to practice after spending several long nerve-racking days in Garmisch waiting for the weather to change. Back in Germany they found the track, though useable, still in pretty poor condition and several competitors were hospitalized during practice. Donna Fox, driver of Team 1, took a nasty spill after negotiating the tricky 'Bayern Curve' in record time when he got into the ruts made by one of the other sleds. He was not seriously injured, but he was badly bruised and on the day competition opened he retired in favor of F W Tyler so as not to jeopardize his team's chances of victory.

Competition began on 11th February for the four-man bobs. The Jury of the Federation sent down three pilot sleds; one spilled, so it was decided not to allow any trial runs due to the still soft foundation of the track. By an unlucky chance Tyler drew the No 1 position on the first day and Kilian, the crack German driver, drew No 1 on the second day; in practical terms this put both teams out of the running since breaking in the track meant losing six to eight seconds on the first run. Tyler still made a remarkably fast time – 1 minute 25 seconds – but it was not nearly fast enough; then, on their second run, the team performed a feat that has gone down in Olympic history and that made them the heroes of the Games. Trying to make up for lost time, Tyler took the Bayern Curve at such a terrific speed that he lost his brake Bickford, who nevertheless managed to hold on with one hand as his body was dragged along the icy curve at somewhere around eighty miles an hour. Lawrence, discovering his plight, reached back and pulled him back into position – a remarkable feat of heroism and fast thinking; the heat was completed in 1 minute 23 seconds.

The second United States sled driven by Hubert J Stevens, holder of the 1932 Olympic two-man championship, had drawn No 15 position. While a bad track on their first run spoiled their chances of winning, they also performed a feat never before equalled in bob-run history and showed real fighting spirit. In negotiating the

dangerous Bayern Curve an unseen hole caused them to swerve so sharply that they spilled on the opposite side into a snowbank; but they righted themselves and carried on so quickly that they ended up in the highly respectable time of 1 minute 25 seconds. The track kept improving and on the following days of competition it was perfect, but the Americans were too far behind to catch up. Switzerland's Team 2 and Team 1 came in first and second and Freddy McEvoy, daring driver for Great Britain, brought his team into third place only 3.56 seconds behind the winner. Stevens finished fourth, 4.28 seconds behind, and Tyler was buried in sixth place.

All the teams spent 13th February, the day before the two-man competitions began, in their special lock-up garages polishing and weighing their sleds and putting them into perfect shape. The morning of the 14th found the track in perfect shape; in the cold weather the foundations had frozen solid and the four pilot sleds made a perfect track. The driver of the United States' Team 1, Ivan Brown, had No 3 position; he realized that he had to get a big lead on the first day in order to win. Both he and Gilbert Colgate, driver of the second sled, made perfect runs, never applying their brakes and bettering all previous track records. It was a grand contest with Brown, Fritz Feierabend, the Swiss driver, and Colgate so close that the winner was in doubt up to the last run. In the end, it was Brown the winner in 5 minutes 29.29 seconds with Feierabend close behind in 5 minutes 30.64 seconds and Colgate trailing with a time of 5 minutes 33.96 seconds.

The German track officials came in for universal praise after the competitions, not only for their fairness

Brown (driver) and Washbond of the American No 1 two-man bob-sled team. They were the Gold Medallists in this competition

but for the colossal effort they had made to get the track into condition; hundreds of men had worked on the run all through each night to get it into peak condition and keep it there.

Another rough-and-tumble sport, ice hockey, provided a surprise winner as Great Britain snatched the Olympic title away from Canada and the United States. The British team, composed mainly of Anglo-Canadians, was challenged by Canada before the competition had even begun; she protested that two of the team members had not fulfilled the residence requirement that would enable them to play for Great Britain. Though petty, the whole affair was very upsetting and caused a certain amount of bad feeling on both sides before Canada eventually withdrew her protest; Britain skated her way through a near fatal match with Germany which ended in a draw after maximum overtime and scored a lucky victory over Canada. In the final pool she beat Czechoslovakia handily and battled her way to a 0–0 draw with the United States until finally her position depended entirely on the outcome of the United States v. Canada game. If America won she and Great Britain would be equal in points and America would win the title by virtue of her superior goal average. But if Canada won Great Britain would have the title free and clear. Canada did win, shutting out the Americans 1–0 and for once the ice hockey championship crossed the Atlantic.

The figure skating competition ended predictably – perhaps too predictably said many critics, who complained that the final placings depended far too much on the personal feelings and patriotism of the judges as well as on the reputation of the skater. The competition was held in a large stadium with an ice surface 100x 200 feet in area; wooden seats accommodating 10,000 spectators completely surrounded the ice. In the men's singles Karl Schafer of Austria easily retained his Olympic championship,

Above : The British ice-hockey team, surprise Gold Medallists as they snatched the title away from Canada and the USA. *Below :* The Canadian ice-hockey team. They challenged the British team before the competition began because it was composed mainly of Anglo-Canadians

Below : The Canada-USA ice-hockey match, upon which the outcome of the contest depended. If America won she would take the Gold Medal from Britain on goal average ; if Canada won Britain would take the medal. In the end Canada won 1-0

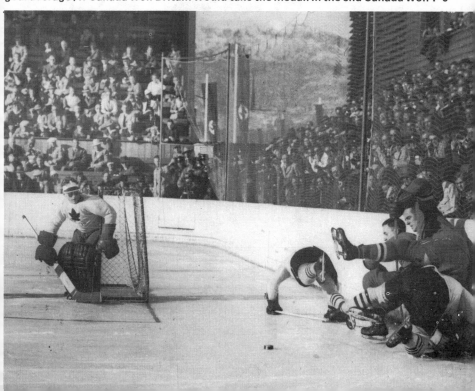

scoring over Germany's Ernst Baier by a comfortable margin. The Americans in the contest were badly bothered by the weather which was cold and windy, with a real blizzard on the second day, as well as by the fact that they were not used to performing on an outdoor rink; the best performances came from 17-year-old Robin Lee of St Paul and Erle Reiter of Minneapolis who finished twelfth and thirteenth. Sonja Henie gave a magnificent exhibition for Norway in the women's singles; her easy finished performance drew a tremendous ovation from the crowd as she retained her Olympic crown for the third time.

In the mixed doubles the German pair, Maxi Herber and Ernst Baier, and the young Austrians, Ilse and Eric Pausin, seemed completely equal, and if the spectators had had their way the Pausins would have won; they danced

Karl Schafer. He retained his Gold Medal for Austria for the men's singles figure skating competition

Sonja Henie. She gave a magnificent exhibition for Norway in the ladies' singles figure skating competition, retaining her Gold Medal for the third time

a difficult program to 'Tales from the Vienna Woods', delighting the judges and audience with their charm and musicality. But the judges were more impressed by the technique of the German couple which was very speedy yet smooth and rhythmic. Much of their program was 'shadow skating' – a very popular style in which the partners execute the same steps in exactly the same way, side by side without touching. The American team, Miss Maribel Vinson of New York City and George Hill of Boston, finished fifth. Although the last part of their program was executed faultlessly, their opening – which consisted of difficult Lutz jumps – did not go as well as planned.

Norway made a clean sweep of the speed-skating competitions, thanks

The ski-jump before the snows set in

A massive firework display near the ski-jump, part of the celebrations to mark the end of the Winter Games

mainly to the efforts of Ivan Ballan-grud. This 32-year-old skater was the undoubted individual star of the contest as he celebrated his participation in three Olympic Games by a triple victory in the 500, 5,000 and 10,000-metre races as well as a second place to his teammate Charles Mathisen in the 1,500-metre event. America's only medal winner was Leo Freisinger, a Chicago boy who came in third in the 500-metre race, 0.7 seconds behind Ballangrud.

Norway, in company with Sweden, also walked away with most of the skiing medals, with the exception of Germany's annexation of the Gold and Silver medals in both the men's and ladies' slalom. Indeed, Christl Cranz, Germany's world champion in the ladies' slalom, lost nineteen seconds by a serious fall, but still managed to win comfortably. Another sensation was the young Norwegian Laila Schou Nilsen, winner of the ladies' downhill race; at only sixteen she was not only a champion skiier, but an excellent speed skater and tennis player as well.

The Winter Olympics left a good taste in the mouths of almost every one who attended them. Gustavus Kirby came home extolling the Games and the spirit that had prevailed in Garmisch. He had noted that the German audience had cheered Rudi Ball at the hockey matches as much as they cheered the Aryan team members and his comments that he had seen absolutely no signs of anti-semitism got very wide publicity in the United States and Europe. Herr von Tschammer und Osten wrote an article for *The Field,* British sporting magazine, in which he gave the German view; he was pleased that the experience at Garmisch had 'melted the ice of pre-judgement' for many of the visitors and recalled with pleasure a 'comrade-ship evening' when 'the men from the USA and our own Storm Troopers in

Birger Ruud, winner of the jumping event in 1932 and again in 1936 for Norway

cheerful surroundings learned to know and appreciate each other'.

The Germans put on several other banquets and entertainments for their guests, including a huge farewell dinner for all the contestants in Munich. Each competitor received an elaborate invitation, a ticket to the ball and a book of coupons entitling him to a ride to Munich on a special train that was met by a brass band, dinner, and suitable souvenirs. More than 2,000 Olympians attended what was generally conceded to be a thoroughly delightful affair. Some American businessmen appreciated Germany as portrayed at the Winter Olympics so much that a worried Berlin correspondent invited the United States commercial attaché to a dinner party in order to enlighten them on the true state of affairs, but the attaché found that he could hardly get a word in

Christl Cranz, winner of the ladies' slalom for Germany in spite of falling in the downhill race

edgeways as the businessmen gleefully told *him* all about Germany. They, like most of the visitors to the Winter Olympics, would probably have agreed with Lord Portal's summing up: 'I feel it my duty to remark that Germany, the German people, the German Organizing Committee and the IOC were fair in every respect and that the Garmisch Games possessed a truly international character. I am convinced that the Germans will be just as fair on the occasion of the Berlin Games, and that this Festival will be carried out in the true Olympic spirit, not only because the IOC and sporting federations demand it, but because the German people wish it.'

Dietrich, Frick, Hitler and Frisch at
Garmisch on the last day of the Winter
Olympics. Most commentators agreed
that the Garmisch Games were a
success, and looked forward to the
Summer Games in Berlin

69

The Olympic Village

When the visitors arrived in Berlin they found that the Organizing Committee had done a truly magnificent job – no finer athletic grounds and arenas had ever before been prepared. Some estimates of the total cost of plant, equipment and operations ran as high as $30,000,000 which contributed in great part to what was to be the greatest athletic spectacle the world had yet seen.

The Olympic Village, especially, came in for much praise. The first time special housing was constructed for Olympic competitors had been in Los Angeles in 1932; the Germans took the idea and expanded and improved upon it, creating a model city for their guests.

It had been originally planned to house the athletes in hotels or in the military barracks at Doberitz. But during the various meetings of the IOC it soon became obvious that most nations would prefer an Olympic Village, and the German Organizing Committee enlisted the help of General von Reichenau, Chief of the War Department, a prominent sportsman who had been associated with the Olympic movement for many years.

The American team marches into the Olympic Village at Berlin, a magnificently planned and constructed model city

He aroused support for the project and on 7th November 1933 the site he had found north of the Hamburg highway was approved as being 'extremely attractive from the standpoint of location and typifying the German landscape'.

The March brothers drew up the plans and the army was put in charge of the construction and organization of the Village, which would be about a fifteen or twenty minute bus ride from the main Olympic stadium. They built 140 houses for the teams, each bearing the name of a German city, laid out in curved rows conforming to the natural contours of the landscape, their cream-colored whitewashed walls and red-tiled roofs sparkling against the dark green of the forest beyond. Interior decor-

Hitler visits the Olympic Village. He was determined that no expense should be spared to make this a tangible expression of the vitality of the new Germany

Set in parkland, the Village was beautifully landscaped, and had been deliberately populated with squirrels who seemed to thoroughly enjoy Village life

ation was the responsibility of a large group of young artists culled from all the schools of fine arts in Germany. Each house contained eight to twelve double bedrooms, a room for each of the house stewards near the entrance, and a compliment of telephone booths, baths, shower rooms and toilets as well as a common room situated in each building so as to provide the best possible view. The bedrooms contained attractive cushions, curtains and hand-woven rugs as well as all the necessary furnishings, and the common rooms were decorated with pictures illustrating life in whichever city the house was named for. In addition, each team was assigned a small office for organizational purposes near one of the restaurants.

The thirty-eight dining halls represented Berlin on the 'map', and a number of small shops and a cinema were scattered throughout the village, as well as a hospital, a post office, exercise fields and facilities for swimming or even just sitting quietly in a small birch wood. Special bird houses, baths and feeding troughs had been scattered liberally through the forest, and the district had been deliberately populated by squirrels who seemed to thoroughly enjoy Village life. Rabbits scampered across the wide lawns, and at the end of the small lake pigeons cooed under the eaves of a sauna while swans drifted across the surface of the water. To complete the idyllic picture workmen had even combed the forest, ruthlessly eradicating every possible breeding ground for mosquitos.

The North German Lloyd Line handled the catering, both for the Village and for Friesen Haus where the women athletes were housed, in their most efficient manner. Comprehensive notes helped the restauranteurs cater for the individual needs of each team. For example, the entry for the United States read: 'Beefsteak as well as lamb and veal daily for lunch and dinner; no fried meat except fowl; underdone steaks before competition; for breakfast, eggs with bacon, ham, oatmeal or hominy, and orange juice; large quantities of fresh or stewed fruit; no kippered herrings; vegetables and baked potatoes with principal meals; sweet dishes including custards and ice cream'. Englishmen, the notes tell us, are 'moderate eaters', while French athletes 'pay less attention to practical nourishment than to tasty and varied dishes'. The Chilean athletes required large quantities of marmalade and the contingent from the Argentine demanded steak à la plancha or empanada à la Creole at least once every day. Milk was the most popular beverage in the Village and the Indian team were the champion milk drinkers, downing an average of two

liters per man per day. The only teams who asked for alcohol were France and Italy, who wanted wine, and Holland and Belgium who requested beer. During the first week of competition the athletes consumed 9,500 lbs of meat each day (more than two lbs per man), but only 1,800 lbs of bread, forty lbs of coffee and 132 lbs of tea.

The food was excellent and varied, and any reasonable demand made through the proper channels was met. The restaurants – open from five in the morning to midnight – could handle 24,000 people and in addition provided food parcels to anyone who requested them. No expense was spared to make the little city perfect; when one of the British officials jokingly remarked that all it needed was a few storks, two hundred birds were conscripted from Berlin immediately! The Reich War Minister, Generaloberst von Blomberg, had ordered an army officer to be assigned to each team as host and advisor.

These men, as well as the 'White Guides' (a group of young people assigned to each team as errand boys and general dogsbodies) came in for much praise from all the teams for their helpful and pleasant attitude during the Games.

Drawbacks to the Village were few and far between. There was no provision made, apparently, for 'breaking training in traditional fashion', as Eleanor Holm Jarrett put it. There was a bit of trouble at first with transportation from the Village to the sports fields which were some distance away, but this was soon ironed out, though the men still envied the women who were within walking distance of the stadium. Unfortunately the inhabitants of Friedrich Friesen Haus were not as happy with their lot. The American women, especially, complained that the rooms were cold, the service bad and the food poor, but representations to the Organizing Committee soon improved matters.

The French team enjoy the excellent cuisine provided by the North German Lloyd Line. Milk was the most popular drink; the only teams to request alcohol were France and Italy (who wanted wine) and Holland and Belgium (beer)

At the previous Olympic Games – in Amsterdam in 1928 and in Los Angeles in 1932 – no arrangements had been made for simultaneous reporting during events; but in 1936 the Germans took care to provide as many facilities as possible and for the first time millions of people in many countries were able to take part in the events.

Some time before the Games began, German language courses were broadcast on short-wave radio; the Berlin stations in their turn ran courses in English, French, Italian and Swedish for the benefit of those citizens in the hotel and restaurant trades or others who were interested. Other foreign broadcasts gave detailed advice on travel in Germany, excursions in and

around Berlin and other items of interest. The periodical *Olympia Dienst*, printed in four languages, enlightened foreign journalists on the arrangements for broadcasting the Games.

Of course the propaganda value of this effort was tremendous, but even setting this aside, the technological achievements alone were impressive. A special allowance of 2,000,000 marks for broadcasting had been made; 400 additional wireless workers were ordered to Berlin in the summer of 1936. The foreign reporters arrived to find 300 microphones, 220 amplifiers and twenty transmitting vans set aside for their use. During the Games ninety-two foreign broadcasters sent reports to nineteen European and thirteen overseas countries, and about as many German broadcasters were on hand reporting to the home audience and assisting those countries that did not have enough reporter coverage in Berlin. Sixty-two reports could be recorded simultaneously and altogether 2,500 reports in twenty-eight languages were transmitted in addition to 500 reports in German.

The efforts of the German broadcasters did not go unnoticed. In their telegram of thanks to Goebbels the foreign broadcasters said 'We leave Berlin filled with admiration for the magnificent achievements of the German radio in the technical no less than in the organizational fields.' And a director of the National Broadcasting Company in America reported that 'the work done by the *Reichsrundfunk* remains without precedent in the history of broadcasting.' Television passed its ordeal by fire as 162,228 fans watched the Games either in one of the twenty-one television auditoriums in Berlin or in similar centres in Potsdam and Leipzig.

Olympic veterans were astonished

The airship *Hindenburg* flies over the Olympic Stadium, which was otherwise free of all aircraft for the duration of the Games

An aerial view of the Olympic Stadium filled with a capacity crowd of 110,000

when they discovered the extent of the set-up in Berlin. Of the nine separate stadiums with a total seating capacity of 237,000, the Olympic Stadium was the largest; it held capacity crowds of 110,000 almost every afternoon during the track and field competitions, and even in the mornings when only trials were being held 60,000 to 80,000 spectators appeared. The swimming stadium held its 18,000 audience during all the contests held there, and nearby Deutschland Hall where the weight-lifting, boxing, wrestling and other indoor gymnastic events were held was crowded most of the time.

The weather throughout the two weeks of the Games was generally cold, dull and damp, but still attendance record; at previous Games were dwarfed at Berlin. Approximately 4,500,000 tickets were sold for the various contests netting a cash return of about $2,800,000 – the greatest income the Games had yet known.

Air space over the stadium was closed to all aircraft with the exception of the *Hindenburg* for the duration of the Games. And, as a final gesture, the Berlin nightclubs that had been closed in Hitler's 'clean-up' campaign were allowed to reopen for six weeks only in order to give the 'degenerate' visitors a taste of Berlin's once-famous night life.

The great test for 'Aryan supremacy'

sang *Deutschland über Alles* and the *Horst Wessel Lied*. The national flags around the rim of the stadium were raised with machine-like precision, and as they unfurled the ten-ton Olympic Bell tolled forth, calling the youth of the world to international friendship through the rivalry of sport.

As if in answer to its call the first of the athletes began to parade into the stadium, led by the Greek team. Other countries followed in alphabetical order, with Germany bringing up the rear. As the French team passed the reviewing stand they delivered the Olympic Salute, despite its similarity to the Nazi Salute and despite the fact that, since the Winter Games, all the participants were well aware of the interpretation Germany would place upon it. They were greeted with tumultous applause, causing one Prussian journalist to comment 'Never was the war threat on the Rhine less than during those moments. Never were the French more popular in Germany than on this occasion. It was a demonstration of comradeship and the will for peace.' It was also a demonstration of the strength of the right wing in a France now, after all, governed by the Socialists under Leon Blum. Unfortunately no uniformity of saluting had been agreed upon by the IOC, so each nation had to decide for itself what form to use. Behind France came Great Britain who, chagrined at the reception given to their Olympic Salute at the Winter Games, delivered a simple 'eyes right'. They were met with almost complete silence.

Several other countries opted out of the Olympic Salute as well, among them Egypt, Argentina, Australia, China, Denmark, Finland and Japan. The New Zealanders and the Belgians doffed their hats and the Americans, resplendent in their white trousers, blue blazers and red white and blue ties, placed their straw boaters over

Saturday, 1st August 1936: the citizens of Berlin and their foreign guests began to gather at dawn and by afternoon the streets were jammed with an excited happy crowd and the sparkling new stadium filled to overflowing. The military band perched on top of the twin towers that flanked the Marathon Gate were tuning up; suddenly they paused, then burst into Wagner's 'March of Homage' as Adolf Hitler passed through the gateway followed by the members of the OIC draped in their glittering chains of office. As he stepped briskly across the ground the five-year-old daughter of the Secretary-General came to great him with the words 'Heil, mein Führer' and presented him with a bouquet of flowers. He patted her cheek, then took his seat as the crowd enthusiastically

As Hitler and the International Olympic Committee pass through the gateway of the new Olympic Stadium a military band bursts into Wagner's 'March of Homage'

their hearts. The gesture was greeted with an outburst of whistling, and Nazi leaders grew pale as the first notes rippled into the air, for whistling is a continental method of showing disapproval; a scene during the opening ceremonies was the last thing anyone wanted. Later, opinion amongst journalists was equally divided, with half of them supporting the view that the Germans in the crowd were upset with the American team and the other half claiming that Americans in the crowd had been supplementing their cheers with whistles. Some German journalists thought that the outburst came because many of their compatriots did not realize that American custom prohibits dip-

The French team marches around the Stadium, giving the Olympic Salute, despite its similarity to the Nazi Salute. They were greeted with tumultuous applause. The British, delivering a simple 'eyes right', were met with almost complete silence

The huge German contingent, all in white, deliver the Nazi Salute to hysterical cheers from the crowd

ping the Stars and Stripes to leaders of other countries; another reporter, who thought he had seen some brown-shirted SA men leading the demonstration, said that it might have been because the Americans, not realizing that Germany had two national anthems, had kept their hats off during the playing of *Deutschland über Alles* but had clapped them on again just as the band swung into the *Horst Wessel Lied*. One lone Costa Rican dipped his flag almost to the ground, and the huge German contingent – dressed all in white and by far the most spectacular sight in the parade – delivered the Nazi salute to hysterical cheers from the crowd.

The athletes arranged themselves in the center of the field and, after a seemingly interminable speech by

Below left : 'I hereby proclaim the Berlin Games of the XI Olympiad Celebrations in the new era as open'. Hitler opens the 1936 Olympiad. The camera has caught Göring halfway into the Nazi Salute. On his left is Leni Riefenstahl, characteristically crouching beside a movie camera for her film *Olympia. Below :* The Olympic Torch begins its twelve-day, 3,000-kilometer journey from Mount Olympus to Berlin. It was carried by 3,000 athletes, each running one kilometer, and the holders were made by Krupp

The Olympic Torch's final stage was run by a Berliner, Schilgen. Tall, slender, golden-haired, and with perfect Nordic features, he entered the Stadium, ran around it, up the stairs at the western end and then ignited the brazier of the Olympic fire which was to burn throughout the Games

Dr Lewald, Head of the German Organizing Committee, Hitler made his official declaration: 'I hereby proclaim the Berlin Games of the XI Olympiad Celebrations in the new era as open.' Amid cheers and a salvo of artillery the Olympic Flag was hoisted, thousands of pigeons were released to carry the news to all corners of the globe and the giant dirigible *Hindenburg* slowly circled the stadium trailing an Olympic Flag.

The Olympic torch had been ignited on Mount Olympus on 20th July and had been carried 2,000 miles to Berlin; the torch relay was another first for the 1936 Games. A member of the British Committee described the scene in the stadium: 'Now at the top of a long flight of steps stood a beautifully proportioned flaxen-haired athlete . . . With dramatic effect he paused, while a gasp of admiration escaped from almost every one of those 100,000 throats. He tripped lightly down the steps holding his torch aloft in his right hand. Half way round the track, for all the world like some athlete from Greek Mythology he ran, and up the steps at the western end. Again he paused; this time to face that vast concourse of people, and then ignited the brazier of Olympic fire which was to burn throughout the Games. As the flames leapt into the air the spectators spontaneously burst into one round of applause.'

As the cheering subsided Loues approached the Führer. This little Greek shepherd had captured the imagination of the world in 1896. All during the course of the first modern Olympic Games Greece had been doing badly while the British and American athletes swept through the events. The last entry on the program was the marathon – the last chance for Greece to make some sort of showing

Spirdon Loues, Greek winner of the Marathon in the first Olympic Games of the new era in 1896, presents Hitler with an olive branch from Mount Olympus

at 'her' Olympic Games. Loues was entered in the marathon – a silent little fellow who had come down out of the hills with a mystic belief that it was his duty to gain this victory for his country. His training methods would not have been exactly recommended by the formidable British and Americans; he fasted during the days before the race and spent most of the preceeding night on his knees in prayer – but at the end it was Loues who trotted into the stadium well ahead of the rest of the pack. Now in 1936 he presented Hitler with an olive branch from Mount Olympus. The flags were dipped as Rudolf Ismayr, a German athlete who had been the weightlifting champion at Los Angeles in 1932, took the Olympic Oath as the representative of all the competitors; finally, a message from Baron de Coubertin, President of the IOC, was relayed over the loudspeakers and the teams filed out to the singing of the *Hallelujah Chorus*. The XI Olympic Games had begun.

The American team was not exactly one big happy family when they arrived in Berlin. As the USS *Manhattan* docked at Hamburg, Avery Brundage had announced that he was regretfully dropping Mrs Eleanor Holm Jarrett from the United States team on charges of breaking training on board ship. Eleanor Holm – an olympic record holder in the women's backstroke division of the swimming competition and odds-on favorite to retain the 100-metre crown – was accused of drinking champagne, smoking and generally carousing during the voyage; an all night party which she attended with Charles MacArthur (but not with his wife, Helen Hayes) was also mentioned in the indictment. She had not heeded hints that she would be better advised to return to the athletes' quarters and finally had been put on probation and given just one more chance, said Brundage. 'I trained on champagne and caviar', replied Mrs Jarrett, who was also a nightclub singer and cine-

The first day. Crowds pour in through the east gate

matic actress, and this assertion was confirmed by her trainers and chaperones. She pointed out that she had given a party the night before the Olympic trials and had still won hands down, but promised that if given the chance she would stop drinking and partying for the duration of the Games. But Brundage was adamant. If there had been only one offence, he replied, he would have considered reversing his judgement, but she had been drinking for a week since his last warning.

The next day she was given separate accommodation and her passage home on the SS *Bremen* at the Committee's expense. The affair caused a furor at home and abroad, as well as among the team members, 220 of whom signed a petition for clemency. Many considered that she was being used as a scapegoat for less conspicuous rule breakers. One of the many telegrams she received expressing support read: 'Abraham Lincoln was informed one day that General Grant was breaking the rules by drinking but nevertheless winning battles. Lincoln's reply in effect was that he wished his other generals would do a little imbibing. Maybe Brundage has forgotten his history. Stick to your guns.' More bad feeling was aroused when she issued a 700-word statement claiming that she was only one in one hundred rulebreakers and was being unfairly singled out, and accusing some of the officials of behaving just as badly. There was a mock marriage and trial aboard ship, she said, and Gustavus Kirby's language was so open to question that some of the athletes left the hall. Kirby of course denied this allegation and approved wholeheartedly of her expulsion from the

Mrs Eleanor Holm Jarrett, Olympic record-holder in the women's backstroke. She was dropped from the American team for breaking training on board ship. A night club singer and film actress, she claimed that she trained on champagne and caviar

team. 'We were all merry and the whole thing was done in the spirit of fun', he claimed.

Eleanor Holm never did sail with the *Bremen*. Instead, a week later, she accepted an American newspaper syndicate's offer to cover the Berlin Games for them. Brundage immediately issued instructions that she was ineligible to compete in any European amateur swimming meets and requested the European organizations to back him up, which they did. He gave no reason for his disqualification, though it would have been possible for him to argue that since she was making money from her standing in sports by reporting on the Olympics she had violated her amateur status. But in America Brundage's high-handed action was seen as lending color to her claim that the penalty imposed for breaking training, which could have been justified, had been carried to the point of personal persecution.

Shortly after the team landed, two boxers, Joe Church of Batavia New York and Howell King of Detroit, were sent home as well. The uproar over the Holm case had made the officials more cautious and they issued the amiable but vague explanation that the men were homesick. Speculation ran rampant – had they too broken training in some way? The boxers, though visibly downcast, insisted that they had not; nor were they victims of homesickness. They claimed that their dismissal was unfair but declined to give any reason for it; it was all a mystery to them, they said, but maybe it was all for the best anyway. And a mystery it remained, for although the American Olympic Committee later alleged that the two men had been caught stealing cameras and had therefore been sent home, others claimed that they had been framed for expressing derogatory opinions about Germany's racial policy while they were shopping in a jewelry store.

By this time relations between officials and athletes had received so much bad publicity that when Sam Stoller and Marty Glickman – both Jews – were removed from the 400-metre relay team an earth-shaking roar of 'Race Prejudice' went up in America. Stoller and Glickman were themselves convinced that it was a political act, but Avery Brundage comments in his report that they were only substitutes, and since they were replaced by two Negroes (Jesse Owens and Ralph Metcalfe) it is hard to make the charge of prejudice stick. It is unfortunate that apart from the justly publicised performance of Jesse Owens, the frequently hard to follow decisions of the American Committee dominated the headlines back home; sports followers read much more about Eleanor Holm Jarrett than about the rest of the aquatic troupe who won their share of prizes, more about the two boxers who were fired than about their teammates who went through with their contests.

The program at Berlin included competition in track and field, wrestling, boxing, modern pentathlon, fencing, rowing, field hockey, weight lifting, soccer, polo, yachting, shooting, handball, basketball, cycling, canoeing, swimming, gymnastics and equestrian events – nineteen sports, not including the women's divisions in track and field, swimming and gymnastics; a record of all the events would fill several thick volumes. It is necessary, therefore, to give but a passing glance to many of the sports and to concentrate on the events in track and field.

The Olympic yachting races were held in Kiel Bay, and the United States team failed to get a first place. In the rowing events on the Grunau course near Berlin the Washington Huskies upheld the tradition that Uncle Sam's boys always come home with the Olympic eight-oared championship. German oarsmen won all the rest of the races except the double sculls which were won for Great

93

The start of the 8-meter class on the second day at Kiel Bay. The United States failed

The Americans win the eight-oared event on the Grunau course near Berlin.
Germany won all the remaining rowing events apart from the double sculls which

There was a dispute when the ranking in the 8-meter class was announced. Finally, on the basis of film taken from a balloon, the Italian team got the Gold Medal, but a tacked-on sail-off was necessary to determine the subsequent ranking – Norway second, and Germany third

Britain by Dick Southwood and Jack Beresford who was competing in his fifth Olympiad. The United States swimming squad just managed to scrape past the Japanese team (who had swept away with the Olympic aquatic championship in Los Angeles in 1932), due mainly to the graceful diving of Marshall Wayne and Dick Degener.

For the second time in Olympic history basketball was on the program. The European officials had adopted a few rules which seemed very strange to the Americans, to put it mildly. For example, a ruling on the maximum height of players disqualified a good part of the United States team. But the game was invented in America and the fundamental principles remained the same; the United States representatives romped over their competitors in fine style as was only to be expected.

The final soccer game between Italy and Austria. Italy won 2-1

Hans Woellke, Germany's shot-put Gold Medallist, her first Olympic champion in track and field since the start of the modern Games in 1896

The soccer competition upheld its record as the most quarrelsome sport on the Olympic chart. In a game between the United States and Italy, players were kicked as often and as hard as the ball; when the German referee tried three times to throw one of the Italians out of the game for deliberate assault and battery he was held down, helpless, by the rest of the team. When assault in soccer goes beyond the recognized rules it bears a striking resemblance to the ancient English game of 'footeball' which numbered its players in hundreds, and the death of a player or two was considered all part of the game. The United States footballers, who did not expect to go very far anyway, just got through the game as quickly and as quietly as they could. Later there was an argument over a match in which

Jesse Owens and Ralph Metcalfe (the 'black auxiliaries' according to the German press) and Frank Wykoff, America's best sprinters, seen training on board ship

Peru beat Austria 4-2. Spectators had invaded the pitch several times during the match and the Jury of the Football Federation ordered a replay. The Peruvians promptly appealed to the IOC who, as it happened, had no jurisdiction in the matter. Exasperated, Peru withdrew her entire team from Berlin. On the other side of the ocean indignant citizens stoned the German consulate, even though the Germans had had nothing to do with the incident, and the Lima longshoremen refused to load German ships at the dock. Later a Jury of Honor of the IOC considered the case and found that the Peruvian team's withdrawal had been the result of a misunderstanding of the rules. They regretted the Peruvian action and deemed it unsportsmanlike. But because of this and similar incidents in the past there was a strong movement to remove soccer from the list for Olympic purposes.

The track and field competition began on Sunday 2nd August. Beneath the twin towers of the Marathon Gate the runners, jumpers and vaulters exercised on the green turf or jogged around the dull red cinder track; spectators were already beginning to whisper that 1936 would be even more of a record-breaking year than 1932.

One of the first events was the shot-put which turned out to be a distinct disappointment to the United States and a source of pride and joy to Germany. Native spectators broke into a frenzy of cheering as Hans Woellke broke the former Olympic record with a throw of 53 feet 1$\frac{13}{16}$ inches, giving Germany her first Olympic champion in track and field since the start of the modern games in 1896. Baerland of Finland was second and Stoeck of Germany third; the United States men, Sam Francis, Jack Torrance

and Dominic Zaitz, finished fourth, fifth and sixth – 'Towering Torrance', vastly overweight, was yards short of the world's record of 57 feet 1 inch that he had set in his earlier thinner days. Hitler watched with enthusiasm and lost no time in calling Woelke to his box for official congratulations.

The next final on the program was the 10,000-metre run and, as everyone expected, it was a clean sweep for Finland. Ilmari Salminen was first to the tape in 30 minutes 15.4 seconds – an unusual performance at these Games in that it set neither a new Olympic nor a new world's record – closely followed by his countrymen Arvo Askola and Volmari Iso-Hollo. Don Lash from Indiana, the United States' best long distance runner, was lost in the pack. Salminen too was promptly led to the official box for congratulations from the Führer.

Meanwhile things were beginning to

Woellke (right) is congratulated by Hitler

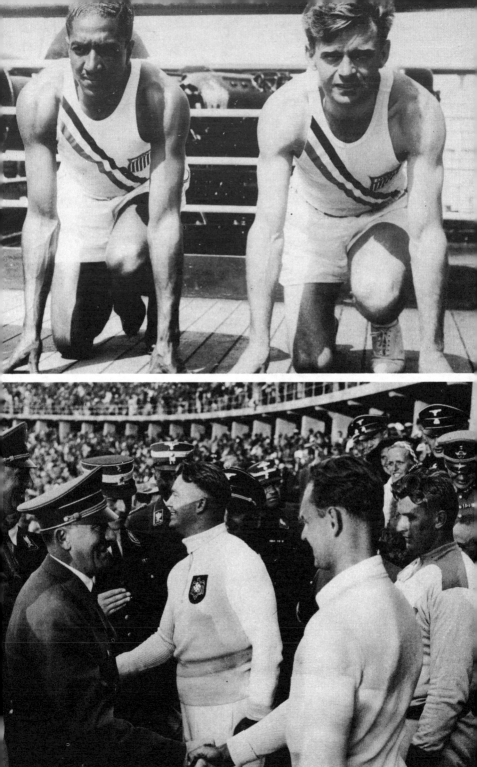

Jesse Owens at the start of the 200-meter event which he won in the record-breaking time of 20.3 seconds

look bad in another quarter as the Negro athletes on the United States' team (the 'black auxillaries', according to *Der Angriff*) began to swing into action. In the semi-final heat of the 100-metre run Jesse Owens, the great sprinter from Ohio State University, won in 10.2 seconds – a new world's record which was however disallowed because of a strong following wind. Ralph Metcalfe, a much blacker auxillary than Owens, stormed through the 100-metre trials and Johnny Woodruff, Negro freshman from the University of Pittsburg, qualified easily in the 800-metre trials along with his white team mates Chuck Hornbostel and Harry Williamson. The Nazi edict that Negroes were an inferior race was not getting a very good run on the cinder path that day, which was further marred by a complaint from the Canadians that the Germans were changing the rules to suit themselves; German officials had ruled that in the trials for the 100-metre dash only the first two men over the finish line should qualify instead of the usual three, thus eliminating Lee Orr, one of Canada's top runners, who finished third in his heat.

But the most embarrassing moment for the Nazis was yet to come; the United States made an unprecedented sweep of the high jump and the winners of the first two places were both Negroes. Cornelius Johnson of California set a new Olympic record of 6 feet 8 inches; Dave Albritton from Ohio State, Delos Thurber of Southern California and Kotkas of Finland cleared 6 feet 6¾ inches, and in the jump-off finished in that order. The eyes of the newspapermen and everyone else in the stadium were glued to

Cornelius Johnson, winner of the high jump at 6 feet 8 inches. Another Negro, David Albritton, was second, and Delos Thurber (also American) was third

Hitler's box. Would he continue his policy of congratulating the winner of each event and publicly shake hands with a black man who had just shown himself superior to several whites? He would not; at that moment he and his retinue were hurriedly leaving the stadium while down on the field Corny Johnson, crowned with the Olympic wreath of victory, grinned.

There are as many versions of this incident as there are people to tell them, but the most probable explanation received by this author comes from K C Duncan, Secretary of the British Olympic Association: after his performance with Woellke and Salminen, says Mr Duncan, Hitler was approached by members of the IOC who told him it was not his place to publicly congratulate winners of any of the events and due to an unfortunate coincidence this happened just before Johnson's victory. The official explanation at the time was that it looked like rain. But of course the incident was tailor-made for those who disapproved of Hitler's racial policies; Herb Flemming, a Negro jazz musician attached to the American team as interpreter, illustrates just what a bad impression it made when he tells how, as Hitler left the stadium, an embarrassed murmur rose from the huge, predominantly German, crowd. And so the first day of track and field competition closed with the story of Hitler's walk-out echoing around the world.

Monday 3rd August saw the weather still cold and unsettled but, nothing daunted, spectators packed the stadium to watch the end of the hammer throw competition, trials in the 3,000-metre steeplechase and 400-metre hurdles, quarter-finals in the 800-metre race and the final of the 100-metre sprint. In the first event of the day Karl Hein of Germany whirled the hammer over his head and hurled it for a distance of 185 feet 4 inches for the championship and a new Olympic record. German members of the audience were ecstatic – here in Berlin, Germany had won a track and field championship on each day of the competition after going without any since 1896. The fact that the promotion of sports for youth was an integral part of the Nazi program made the victories all the sweeter. Another German, Erwin Blask, was second in the hammer throw and Oskar Warngard of Sweden third. The event had been a United States' monopoly until 1928, but her showing on this day was somewhat substandard; Bill Rowe of Rhode Island State finished fifth. Don Favor of Portland Missouri was sixth, and Harry Dreyer of the New York Athletic Club did not even make the final.

Other United States athletes were making better progress in their events. Joe McCluskey, Harold Manning and Glen Dawson qualified in the steeplechase trials; the leaders in the three 'quarter-finals' for the 800-metre race were Chuck Hornbostel, John Woodruff and Harold Williamson. In the 400-metre hurdles Glenn Hardin, Joe Patterson and Dale Schofield qualified with no trouble at all. Jesse Owens broke the tape in the first semi-final of the 400-metre event with Frank Wykoff right behind him; Ralph Metcalfe won the second semifinal. Hans Strandberg of Sweden, Erich Birchmeyer of Germany and Martin Osindarp of Holland were the starters, along with Owens, Metcalfe and Wykoff for the United States in the 100-metre final. 'The Tan Streak from Ohio State', who was not usually a fast starter – he preferred to catch up and pass his opponents half-way through the race – took a deep breath of that Olympic air, and at the crack of the gun he was off. He was followed by Wykoff and Osindarp with Big Ralph Metcalfe running a poor last. They flashed down the track, Owens holding his lead and Metcalfe madly cutting down the men ahead of him. He caught all of them except Owens; as they sped over the finish line he was barely a metre behind. Osindarp finished third, about a metre behind

Metcalfe, with Wykoff, Borchmeyer and Strandberg following in that order.

Even on that soggy rainsoaked track Owens had equalled the Olympic record of 10.3 seconds. This was the first hint of anything superlative; Owens seemed in a class by himself as he ran, arms and legs working in perfect rhythm, in his effortless style. No one had any doubt that they were watching sheer athletic genius. Metcalfe got his revenge later; on 10th August, after the track and field competitions in Berlin were over, he managed to outrun Owens in an exhibition match in Cologne.

Hitler, meanwhile, was carefully keeping well within the bounds laid down by the IOC. He did congratulate Hein and Blask on their victory in the hammer throw, but he did it privately in quarters underneath the stands. But of course public opinion outside Germany put the worst possible construction on his motives.

Next day, 4th August, was a gala day for the USA. The weather was bleak as the 'black auxillaries' turned out in force; 9,000 spectators braved the cold and wet to watch the morning trials. A capacity crowd of 110,000 was on hand for the three final events in the afternoon. Foreigners in Berlin were constantly amazed to see how the Germans flocked to the various events; the Olympic fever had such a hold on them that they would turn out in hordes to watch anything and everything, whether they understood it or not. In the course of the Games two amateur baseball teams from the United States put on an exhibition game that would have been lucky to pull 200 people into the Polo Grounds in New York City. In Berlin where no one knew anything about baseball, it drew 100,000 baffled spectators to the Olympic Stadium one night – up to that time the largest crowd ever to see a ball game anywhere.

Glenn Hardin of Mississippi had no competition in the 400-metre hurdle the tall curly-haired easy-going Southerner breezed to victory in 52.4 seconds, well short of the Olympic record that he had set himself in 1932 of 52 seconds flat. (In that race he finished second to Bob Tisdale of Ireland, but Tisdale's time of 51.8 was disallowed because he knocked over the last hurdle.) Joe Patterson of the US Navy stuck with Hardin in the beginning of the race, but faded in the stretch to finish fourth behind John Loaring of Canada and Miguel White of the Philippines.

But it was the 'Charge of the Black Brigade' which left the great crowd gasping, led brilliantly by Jesse Owens. He and Mack Robinson were up early for the trials in the 200-metre dash along with their white running mate Bob Packard. Packard won his heat and later qualified in his quarter-final. Robinson not only won his heat, but tore through his quarterfinal like a fourth of July rocket to equal the Olympic record of 21.2.

But it was Owens, the 'Buckeye Bullet', who was the tornado that day. First he won his trial heat in 21.1, breaking both the Olympic and world's records for the distance. Then he sauntered over to the jumping pit for the running broad jump trials – just a formality since he already held the world's record. He was jogging down the track, still wearing his sweater, to test the road conditions, when suddenly the red flag went up. This was to be considered an official jump even though he had not jumped at all! On his second try he made a good jump and seemed to be well past the qualifying mark, but the red flag went up again; he had overstepped the take-off. Only one more jump. And if he made any error at all the athlete who was acknowledged to be the greatest broad jumper in the world would be out of it at the start. But after his third jump the worried United States officials breathed a sign of relief; he made no error and qualified easily.

That afternoon Jesse sizzled over the cinders for 200-metres in 21.1

Jesse Owens gains another Gold Medal for the broad jump, setting a new world and Olympic record of 26 feet 5¼ inches

to win his quarterfinals section. So he was already the Olympic champion in the 100-metre dash and had broken two Olympic records in one day. Looking as fresh as when he had started, he strolled back to the broad jump pit. He had no competition from any of the other jumpers and was well in the lead, until Germany's entry, Lutz Long, shot down the runway and equalled his mark. When Long's distance was announced the crowd roared happily, but their jubilation was short-lived; Jesse calmly and methodically sped down the track, hit the take-off mark and soared through the air. He came down a fraction over 26 feet from the mark; the first 26-foot jump in Olympic history. In his final jump, Long, in his anxiety to beat Owens, fouled out; but Owens cleared 26 feet 5¼ inches, breaking the Olympic record

for the second time that afternoon. In this battle of the jumping giants the previous Olympic record had been beaten five times and equalled once. The smiling soft-spoken college student had himself surpassed former Olympic records four times and a world's record twice. He had gained his second Olympic crown and, from his performance in the 200-metre trials, it seemed certain that a third was on the way; something of a slap in the face for the advocates of Aryan aristocracy. Hitler called Long to his private quarters under the stands and congratulated him, as foreign newspapers gleefully pointed out, on performing the magnificent feat of finishing second to a foreigner and a Negro. But Long's performance cannot be

Lutz Long, Germany's best broad jumper. Hitler called him to his private quarters under the stands and congratulated him (as foreign newspapers pointed out) for coming a gallant second to a foreigner and a Negro

denegrated for it really was in the best tradition of athletics and sportsmanship; not only had he jumped further than any German in the history of the Olympics and himself beaten the previous Olympic record, but Owens claimed later that it was a tip from Long that made it possible for him to achieve his last spectacular distance.

The 800-metre final can only be described as an astonishing race. Woodruff, Williamson and Hornbostel represented America. Their most formidable opponents were Mario Lanzi of Italy, Kazimierz Kucharski of Poland and Phil Edwards, the Canadian veteran. The rest of the starters were Juan Anderson of the Argentine, Gerald Backhouse of Australia and Brian MacCabe from Great Britain. Woodruff was a tall spare solemn-looking young Negro who had risen from obscurity to the top ranks of track athletics in two months. He was inexperienced and knew little about pace and strategy; he changed his gait and direction more times than a driver changes gears in the rush hour. Head Coach Lawson Robertson had told Woodruff to get out in front and stay there in order to keep himself clear of possible trickery or trouble, but this is just what Woodruff did not do. Phil Edwards was off in the lead and Woodruff found himself in a pocket near the rear of the pack.

For nearly a lap he tried to dodge his way out of the trap, but he was completely blocked by the arms and legs of his rivals. So he adopted a bizarre bit of strategy to get out of the spot and came to almost a full stop in the middle of the track. This desperate measure cleared up his traffic problem immediately, since all the others simply ran off and left him, free and clear at the end of the

procession. And then Woodruff started to run. Thrashing his legs around in what looked like several directions at once, the Pitt freshman took the outside at a furious pace, and in 100 metres he had caught and passed the whole pack. There he was, roaring along in front, but that wild sprint had cost him something and he was just having a little breather in the back stretch when Phil Edwards snuck up and took the lead again. As they hit the final turn Mario Lanzi came up fast on the outside and Woodruff was trapped again. Around the last corner they went in a grim struggle with Edwards directly ahead of Woodruff and Lanzi blanketing him on the outside, with a great amount of barging and boring going on among the three of them. But as they came into the stretch Woodruff took what seemed to be a running broad jump on a tangent to get clear of Lanzi, sailed past Edwards, and in a couple of strides was off on his own, heading for the tape with a five-metre lead.

Then, just when it looked to everyone as if he had the race all tied up he began to sag; the traffic jams, the extra distance he had run and the terrific sprints he had put on at different stages had taken their toll. Lanzi saw this; here was his chance to grab a victory for Italy under the very eyes of Prince Umberto who was up in Hitler's box cheering him on. He speeded up, giving it everything he had; he passed Phil Edwards and began to catch up to the now faltering Woodruff. As they pounded down the track he drew closer - four metres, three, two . . . but that was as close as he could get before they reached the tape. Woodruff's time of 1 minute 52.9 seconds was not very good compared to other marks made at Berlin that year, but it wasn't at all bad when his zig-zag course and stop-and-go style are taken into consideration. The general consensus of opinion was that after 'Wandering Woodruff' learned to use his head as well as his legs, 1 minute 48 seconds or under

The victory ceremony for the winners of the broad jump – Naoto Tajima (Japan, third), Jesse Owens (USA, first) and Lutz Long (Germany, second)

would be well within his grasp.

The 5,000-metre trials were held on Tuesday as well. Of the United States contingent Louis Zamperini had to sprint desperately to gain fifth, the last qualifying place in his heat, and Tommy Dechard missed qualifying altogether. Don Lash got a comfortable third in his heat, but none of it mattered in the end anyway. In the final on Friday Lash and Zamperini were left far behind as the tireless Finn, Gunnar Hoecker, ran away to finish in 14 minutes 22 seconds.

On Wednesday 5th August the stadium was jammed as usual. The weather was chilly and showery for the fifth consecutive day, but Jessie Owens was going for the triple crown and no one, native or tourist, was going to miss the spectacle. For by this time Owens was a hero on the streets of Berlin as well as a marvel on the cinderpath; the Germans had accepted him as an athletic genius and were really enthusiastic over his remarkable performances. A few Nazi newspapers like *Der Angriff* made cutting comments about the American slump in sports, since up to that time the only white winner on the squad had been Glenn Hardin. But black or white, United States athletes had won five of the eight events completed so far with more triumphs yet to come.

There were several minor matters to occupy the attention of the spectators before the main event in the afternoon. In the morning there were trials in the 1,500-metre race, the 110-metre hurdles, the pole vault, and the discus. All of the United States men came through as expected, but they received a distinct shock in one of the heats of the 1,500-metre event. In 1934 and 1935 Jack Lovelock, a Rhodes Scholar from New Zealand, had repeatedly beaten America's best milers, Bill Bonthron and Glenn Cunningham. The last time they had met at Princeton he had won so easily that it was taken for granted that this slim sandy-haired medical student was far and away the best miler in the

world. But in the autumn of 1935 and the spring of 1936 Lovelock had been beaten four times in five races by Sydney Wooderson, a lanky bespectacled barrister's clerk in England. And Wooderson, in a mild way, was the sensation of Berlin. Unknown to the spectators he had damaged an ankle in training; he bogged down to the stretch of his 1,500-metre heat and the crowd saw the much heralded sensation from England walk home in ninth place. It was a disappointment, since he was a great runner, probably the greatest miler of the 30s. But even with Wooderson out the 1,500-metres promised a few thrills. From the United States Glenn Cunningham, Archie San Romani and Gene Venzke had qualified easily. There was always Lovelock, and a distinct threat was looming in the shape of Luigi Beccali, the dark handsome Italian with the determined jaw who had won at Los Angeles in 1932.

Meanwhile the 50-kilometre walkers had set out on their tour of Berlin and the surrounding landscape, and the semi-final heats of the 200-metre race were run off. Bob Packard was shut out of his heat, but Mack Robinson won his in 21.1, a tenth under the Olympic record set by squat little Eddie Tolan at Los Angeles: Owens strolled through his semi-final in 21.3.

The pole vault had settled into a contest between three Southern Californians – Earl Meadows, Bill Graber and Bill Sefton – and two lithe athletes from Japan, Shuhei Nishida and Sugo Oe. The Americans remembered Nishida well – he had come to within an inch of Bill Miller's title-winning jump at Los Angeles. Rain began to drizzle dolefully down and the approach to the vaulting pit was a quagmire, but as the rain came down the athletes kept going up. Finally, when the bar was an inch below 14 feet Bill

The 50-kilometer walkers set out on their tour of Berlin and the surrounding countryside. Harold Whitlock of Britain won in 4 hours 30 minutes 41.1 seconds

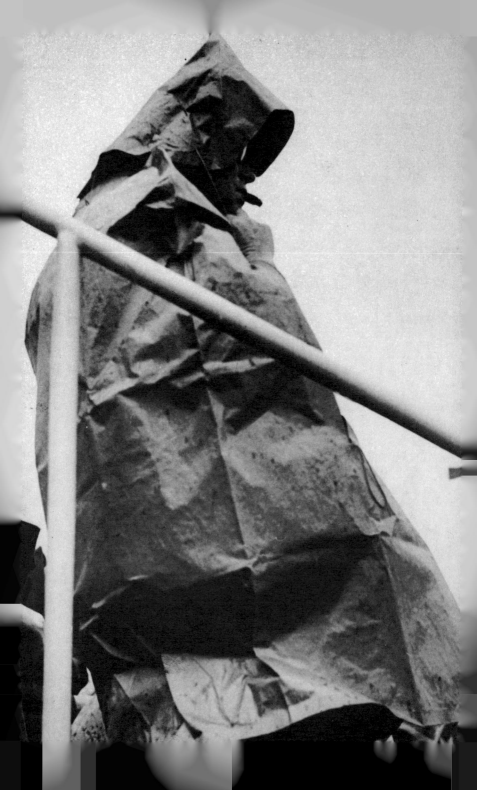

Graber missed, and the other four were left to carry on the struggle.

As the rain got heavier the darkness deepened until, in gloom so thick that spectators at the top of the stadium could hardly see them, each vaulter tried 4.35 metres – and missed. On the second time around Earl Meadows wriggled over, just brushed the bar, and landed on his back in the pit. He stared upwards into the dark . . . and the bar stayed put. At just a fraction under 14 feet 3 inches it was a new Olympic record and a good inch over Bill Miller's 1932 jump. Then all Meadows had to do was sit in a puddle and wait for the other three to try and catch up to him. Each had two attempts; each tried once and failed. One more round to go; Sefton kicked the bar off when he went over and on his last try Oe made the height but brushed the bar off with his chest. The crowd cheered the final contender through the dusk: 'Nishida!' Nishida!' they chanted rhythmically. At the end of the runway Nishida smiled, raised his pole and moved swiftly down the soggy path. Up with a whirl and a heave – but his elbow hit the bar on the way over. Earl Meadows was the new Olympic champion and record holder. In the jump-off Sefton finished second and Nishida and Oe, still tied for third and fourth, decided to call it a day and divide the honor later at home.

There were no surprises in the 110-metre hurdle trials, though there was a moment of doubt when the top-ranked man, Forrest Towns, stumbled between the second and third hurdles. But he quickly recovered and won easily. Other United States hurdlers who qualified were Fritz Pollard Jr, son of the great Brown footballer of previous years, and Roy Staley. The soggy spectators sitting in the cold dark stadium straightened up. The big

A spectator determined not to get as wet as many of the competitors did during the drizzly weather which hampered record-breaking

event of the day, the 200-metre race, was about to begin. Just as the six runners lined up at the starting mark, the 50-kilometre walkers began to filter back into the stadium. Great Britain's Harold Whitlock was first over the line and his announced time of 4 hours 30 minutes 41.4 seconds was received with thundering apathy, even though it was a new world's record. No one in the drenched crowd paid any attention to the rest of the pedestrian arrivals and once more the sprinters crouched at the starting mark. In the line-up were Owens, Robinson, Osendarp, Lee Orr of Canada, Paul Haenni of Switzerland and Wynand van Beveren from Holland. Jesse Owens had the race all to himself; from the bark of the starting gun he was off in front and crossed the finish line all alone in 20.7 seconds, smashing the old Olympic record and setting a new world's record in the bargain. Mack Robinson, breathing heavily, followed three or four metres behind with Osendarp plugging away at his shoulder to take third place.

So in the gloom of this murky evening Jesse Owens completed his triple triumph and the bedraggled spectators rose up to pay tribute to the individual hero of the Berlin Games. Hitler, a most persistant observer, had braved the inclement weather to watch this feature event. He saw Owens gallop home to win his third crown and he watched Mack Robinson capture second place – another one-two victory for the black auxillaries. Native Nazis as well as tourists sent up a thunder of applause as Jesse stood on the victor's block to receive his reward.

The ceremony for crowning Olympic victors was very picturesque. The three victors lined up on a pretty tribune wreathed in evergreen and gold in front of the Führer's box where the guests of honor surrounded Hitler. The first place winner stood in the center slightly raised above the silver medallist on his right and the bronze on his left. As they faced the Führer

Undaunted by the rain, a capacity crowd
watches the final of the handball event.
1936 was the sole occasion that this event, a
central European game rather like rugby
football, was in the Olympic program.
Germany won the Gold Medal

and the little band of Olympic officials headed by Count Henri de Baillet-Latour the band's trumpets at the end of the stadium sounded a fanfare and the whole stadium rose to its feet. Three girls in white uniforms chosen for their grace and beauty came forward and as the victors leaned toward them they crowned them with chaplets of laurels. The first place winner also got a pot containing a tiny oak tree. The loudspeaker proclaimed each man's name and victory, the scoreboard at the end of the stadium flashed it out and the band struck up the national anthem of the victor while the athletes stood at attention (the Germans usually with outstretched arms). The crowd remained standing for the anthem and then cheered their heads off as the beautiful maidens, in perfect alignment, retired to the sidelines and the victors stepped down, saluted the box and walked away. This could get to be a very long drawn out procedure if there were many German winners, for then both *Deutschland über Alles* and the *Horst Wessel Lied* had to be played and sung with fervor each time, but in all cases it was a very stirring proceeding.

But when Jesse Owens climbed onto the tribune he faced the Olympic Committee, but not Herr Hitler. Just after he had crossed the finish line the drizzle had turned into a downpour and Hitler and his retinue had hurriedly departed. This was perhaps a sensible proceeding in view of the weather, but there were more than enough clucking tongues to gloat that the powerful apostle of Nordic supremacy had been driven from his own stadium in his own beautiful city of Berlin into sudden retreat by a mild-mannered Negro from Cleveland.

Meanwhile, the spectators learned, Ken Carpenter of California had won the discus event, whirling the steel platter out for a distance of 50.48 metres, or 165 feet 7 29/64 inches – another new Olympic record. His team mate Gordon Dunn, another Californian, was four feet and a frac-

tion behind him with Giorgio Oberweger of Italy placing third by a matter of inches.

Germany produced a startling surprise on Thursday, 6th August when Gerhard Stoeck won the javelin throw, an event which had previously been monopolized by Sweden and Finland. The Finn Matti Jarvinen was competing at Berlin and this world's record holder was expected to win by a comfortable margin. But Jarvinen was off his best form and the crowd went mad as Stoeck's winning throw of 71.84 metres was announced. Yro Nikkanen and Kaarlo Toivonen, both from Finland, placed second and third. The best effort for the United States was made by Alton Terry who placed sixth with a toss of just over 220 feet – not bad for an American, but not nearly good enough to meet the foreign competition.

Naoto Tajima won the hop-step-and-jump for Japan, clearing 52 feet 5 5/16 inches; another Japanese, Masao Harada was a bit over a foot

behind him in second place. This was the third time in succession that Japan had won this event; Roland Romerio was the only American to make the final round and he finished fifth.

In the morning the trials for the 400-metre relay event were held. Great Britain had a great trio entered, A G K Brown, Bill Roberts and a seasoned veteran, Lieutenant Godfrey Rampling. Against them the United States had put Archie Williams, Jimmy LuValle and, despite a threatened attack of appendicitis, Hall Smallwood. Smallwood had spent the voyage to Germany tucked up in bed with an ice pack, but he did not run like an invalid this day; all of the Big Six made it easily through their trials.

The 1,500-metre final that afternoon has gone down as one of the greatest races in the Olympic annals and in track and field history. All of the twelve starters were great runners and the greatest of these were Luigi

Jack Lovelock (in black), winner of the 1,500-meter final for New Zealand in 3 minutes 47.8 seconds. It was a splendid race which has gone down in track and field history

Beccali, Olympic winner of 1932, Glenn Cunningham, world's record holder for the mile, and John Lovelock, the New Zealander who had repeatedly beaten Cunningham and Bill Bonthron in great matches in America. There were other potentially dangerous runners in there like young Archie San Romani and Gene Venzke of the United States, Miklos Szabo of Hungary and Erik Ny of Sweden. The veteran Negro Phil Edwards was in for Canada. There was the steady-going Englishman Jerry Cornes. But Beccali, Cunningham and Lovelock were the men to watch; another episode in the Cunningham-Lovelock rivalry was in itself exciting enough to make the trip and admission fee worthwhile. The last time they had met at Princeton in Palmer Stadium in 1935 the pleasant interne from London with the curly red hair had run Cunningham into the ground. Today 'Galloping Glenn' was out for revenge.

As the runners stopped jogging about and began to remove their jerseys and pullovers a hush fell over the huge crowd. They lined up, some setting themselves for a crouching start while others clung to the old-fashioned start, merely leaning forward, semi-erect, with their hands poised to help with an initial swing. When the gun barked the English veteran Jerry Cornes broke into the lead and almost a full lap had been completed before the runners had settled in their stride. The Big Three – Cunningham, Lovelock and Beccali – were watching each other and not bothering too much about the leadership; when Cornes dropped back Shaumberg of Germany was allowed to take the lead. Then Beccali began to move up. Cunningham swung wide and went into the lead with Lovelock sticking right on his heels. But at the beginning of the final lap Ny of Sweden and Shaumberg sprinted up and wedged themselves between Cunningham and Lovelock, trapping Lovelock in fourth place. As they went into the lower turn Ny turned on another burst of speed and moved in front as Shaumberg began to fade. Lovelock was in third place, once again on Cunningham's heels; Beccali was gliding quietly along in fourth and Archie San Romani had come up from nowhere to join the leaders in the last whirl.

Then at the lower end of the backstretch the slim New Zealander – he had never weighed more than 135 pounds in his life – made his move. He slipped past Cunningham, then past Ny and was in the lead, a wispy figure in a black running suit. Had he started his sprint too soon? If so, sturdier runners like Cunningham and Beccali could cut him down for his mistake. Beccali and Cunningham whirled past the sagging Swede and took off after Lovelock. Around the upper turn they fled, and into the final straight, the defending Olympic champion in third, the world's record holder in second and, way out in front, the Rhodes Scholar from New Zealand drifting along as if his feet did not need to touch the ground. Beccali burst into the sprint that had clinched his 1932 victory, but this time it was not good enough – Cunningham had called on his last ounce of strength and was flashing down the track in the greatest sprint of his career. But Lovelock, amazingly, was going even faster with what looked like complete ease. As he neared the tape he glanced over his shoulder, saw his pursuers far behind, and coasted over the finish line in 3 minutes 47.8 seconds – one full second under the listed world's record for 1,500 metres set by Princeton's 'Bounding Bill' Bonthron in 1934. He had carried the field so fast that the next four men behind him – Cunningham, Beccali, San Romani and Edwards – were all ahead of the former Olympic record for that distance. Jesse Owens' triple triumph was the greatest accumulation of glory by any individual athlete at Berlin, but this record-making run by Lovelock was certainly the greatest single feat performed on any one day in a great week of competition.

Next morning, 7th August, was given over to the decathalon events, with Jack Parker, Bob Clark and Glen Morris from the United States gaining a lead that discouraged all the other entrants. In the afternoon came the semi-finals of the 400-metre race, with eligibles including the United States trio of Smallwood, Williams and LuValle, and the British Big Three consisting of Roberts, Brown and Rampling. Harold Smallwood was the first victim and he was out before the starting gun went off – while his rivals were running around the track in the stadium Hal was lying in a bed in a Berlin Hospital having his appendix out at last. The second victim was Lieutenant Rampling who was shut out in the second semifinal. The stars from the United States led in both tests; in the first Williams won, with Bill Roberts second and Johnny Loaring of Canada third, while in the second LuValle was the leader followed by Brown and Bill Fritz of Canada. It would be an English-speaking final.

From the crack of the gun starting the final in the 400-metres all eyes were on Brown and Williams. Brown, a Cambridge University undergraduate, was a sprinter who could run 'the hundred' in well under even time; he took the lead with Williams and LuValle hot on his trail. Williams caught up and passed him as they turned into the straight but LuValle never quite made it. The excitement in the final stretch was terrific, with Brown slowly and steadily closing the gap and Williams striving desperately to hold on to his diminishing lead until he could reach the finish line. At one point Brown seemed to draw almost level with Williams; at another he was a yard behind. But despite his efforts Williams crossed the line first. Williams' time was 46.5 seconds, with Brown but a stride behind him and Luvalle and Roberts third and fourth respectively, so close together that the watches caught them both at 46.8 seconds; the two Canadians finished fifth and sixth.

Don Lash and Louis Zamperini represented the United States in the 5,000-metre field; Lash, a chunky tow-headed youngster from Indiana, thought he might have a chance if he was anywhere near the front in the last lap. But as usual the Flying Finns had things their own way and Lash was left far behind. Ilmari Salminen, who had won the 10,000-metre race on the first day of competition was in front with his team mates Lauri Lehtinen, winner at Los Angeles in 1932, and Gunnar Hoeckert, with John Henry Jonsson of Sweden and Kohei Murakoso of Japan clinging stubbornly to their heels. The Finns were apparantly headed for a 1-2-3 sweep when suddenly, with only a lap to go, there was a traffic jam among the leaders. Salminen tumbled to the ground and the others ran off and left him; Hoeckert won in the Olympic record time of 14 minutes 22.2 seconds, followed by Lehtinen, Jonsson and Murakoso. Murakoso, in fourth place, equalled the former Olympic record of 14 minutes 30 seconds that Lehtinen had set at Los Angeles against Ralph Hill of Oregon.

Now the program was drawing to a close and, the American athletes had captured most of the honors in track and field. Four Negroes had won six events for the USA and four more had been won by their white team-mates. The United States had won eleven Gold Medals at Los Angeles and fans hailed it as a glorious victory. Now, at Berlin, amid competition that shattered old Olympic records in all directions, that victory would be surpassed.

On Saturday, 8th August the complicated program of the decathlon was finished and after some hasty calculations the statisticians declared a victory for the United States. The winner was Glenn Morris, a husky 24-year-old automobile salesman from Fort Collins, Colorado who set a new Olympic record of 7,900 points by the revised table. In second place was Bob Clark of San Francisco, and Jack Parker of Sacramento finished third to round off the victory.

The record-breaking continued in the other important event of the day, the 3,000-metre steeplechase, but the United States had nothing to do with it. The hero was Volmari Iso-Hollo of Finland who managed to set two records at the same time; his time of 9 minutes 3.8 seconds was an Olympic record and his successful defense of the Olympic title he had won four years before was a Berlin record - in fact he was the only athlete to gain the distinction of retaining his own title. The United States had Harold Manning, Joe McClusky and Glenn Dawson in that race, but the Finns left them far behind. Even so, Man-

Volmari Iso-Hollo, winner of the 3,000-meter steeplechase in a world record time of 9 minutes 03.8 seconds. He was Gold Medallist in this event at Los Angeles in 1932

ning, who finished fifth, was under the old Olympic record and had the best time ever recorded for an American runner over an Olympic steeplechase course. Glenn Dawson finished eighth and Joe McClusky finished tenth. The crowd showed little excitement as the Finns moved on toward almost certain victory, but then Alfred Dompert of Germany began to move up, becoming a determined threat. Hitler stood up and yelled with excitement and the crowd roared wild cheers as Dompert rushed furiously along. Iso-Hollo was well in the lead and had no fears of being overtaken, but Dompert plunged past Martii Matilainen to spoil Finland's sweep and headed after Kaarlo Tuominen who had thought that he had the Silver Medal securely in his pocket. Tuominen managed to win the battle for second place only by a couple of strides.

On Sunday, with the running of the two relays and the marathon, the track and field competitions at the 1936 Berlin Olympics came to an end. Many in the United States camp were worried about the 1,600-metre relay since Britain's Big Three were entered in the event. But Head Coach Lawson Robertson was thinking about the German and Italian competitors in the 400-metre relay and to this end he pulled Sam Stoller and Marty Glickman out of the team and replaced them with Jesse Owens and Ralph Metcalfe.

Jesse Owens and Ralph Metcalfe in the 400-meter relay, won by the Americans in a new world record of 39.8 seconds. Owens and Metcalfe had substituted for Sam Stoller and Martin Glickman, the only Jews in the American track and field squad. The substitution was badly timed, and accusations of predudice hung over the American coaching staff for years

The start of the Marathon

As expected the United States walked away with the race, setting an Olympic and world's record of 39.8 seconds. Germany came in second and the Italians had to be satisfied with third. But the team had had no chance to practice together and their stick handling was extremely sloppy. Glickman and Stoller remained convinced that if they had been allowed to run they could have done just as well.

Critics who had blasted Robertson's substitution in the 400-metre relay team wondered why he had not switched the 1,600-metre team about, since they were the more vulnerable, and put in Archie Williams and Jimmy LuValle. With Brown and Roberts in Great Britain's team it was clear that the British would be more than just a threat. Robbie replied that while Owens and Metcalfe were willing and able to run in the short race, Williams and LuValle were worn out and did not

want to compete in the longer one. There was really no competition as Brown, Roberts and Rampling, along with their starter Frederick Wolff, coasted to the tape with a comfortable margin in 3 minutes 9 seconds, well ahead of Harold Cagle, Bob Young, Eddie O'Brien and Al Fitch on the US team.

Meanwhile, at three o'clock the marathon runners set out on their long trek. Juan Carlos Zabala, a former newsboy in the Argentine who had won in 1932, led the fifty-six runners, clad in all sorts of colours and costumes, along the stadium track and out through the 'marathon tunnel' It was a hot day and the perspiring runners could not have been helped by the sight of German families sitting in shaded beer gardens along the route sipping lager as the course wound through the rural district around the River Havel. One estimate calculated that about 1,000,000 spectators saw some part of the marathon race as the troupe toiled over the

hard macadam roads under the warm sun. Ellison (Tarzan) Brown, the only Indian on the United States team, was the leading American entrant; but some days earlier an exercise session with one of the 50-kilometre walkers had left his heels horribly sore and it was suspected that he would not last the distance. The suspicion proved to be well founded. At ten kilometres the loudspeaker in the stadium reported that Zabala was still proudly in the lead, Manuel Diaz of Portugal was second and Brown was third, with Ernest Harper of Great Britain and Kitei Son of Japan treading close on his heels. At twenty-one kilometres (about half way through the ordeal) Zabala was still clinging to his lead, but Diaz had dropped back and Tarzan Brown had disappeared altogether.

As they jogged along together behind Zabala, Harper reassured Keiti

Kitei Son of Japan and Ernest Harper of Britain in the lead at the halfway stage of the Marathon

Kitei Son's triumph in the Marathon, the last track and field event of the 1936 Games

Son; Zabala would be folding soon, there was no need to worry about him. The dogged Englishman was right. At thirty-one kilometres Zabala began to slow up and at thirty-two kilometres he sat down and took off his shoes. The slim Korean-born student from Tokyo University took the lead and at thirty-seven kilometres began to pull away from Harper. Soon after this news had been broadcast to the stadium spectators, the crowd was taken by surprise as the little yellow-skinned runner clad in white popped out of the marathon tunnel and began trotting towards the finish line. Their tribute, though delayed, was enthusiastic as the 21-year-old youth finished his long run in an Olympic record breaking time of 2 hours 29 minutes 19.2 seconds, with no visible signs of fatigue. Then he sat down beside the track, took off his shoes and trotted quietly off to his dressing room. He had disappeared before Harper, a 29-year-old miner from Sheffield, came through the tunnel followed by Shoryu Nan, another Korean-born student running for Japan, and the rest of the field. One by one they filtered into the stadium through the twilight, and the track and field competition of the XI Olympic Games was over.

The United States had outstripped all her opponents in track and field; using the conventional scoring method (ten points for each first place, five for each second, and four, three, two or one for third through sixth places), the team had managed to accumulate a grand total of 203 points. Finland, in second place, had only 80¼ points, and Germany came third with 69¾. Germany, however, used a different scoring system and many

The Olympic flags are lowered as a choir and orchestra perform Paul Hoeffer's 'Farewell to the Flag'

American newspapers took exception to her claim that she was the leader in the Olympic contest. The German method was to count the total number of medals earned; Germany had 46 – 13 Gold, 16 Silver and 17 Bronze, while America only had 32 (15 Gold, 11 Silver and 6 Bronze) and Finland and Sweden were tied for third place with 17 medals each. 'This is not a style of figuring that appeals to true Olympians', the *New York Times*, declaimed, noting that several of Germany's medals had been won for city planning, architecture, music, literature and art. They conveniently forgot to mention that if scores were to be calculated on the basis of *all* sports events so far completed, Germany would still be ahead with 310 1/4 points as opposed to America's 272 1/2, Finland's 119 1/4 and Sweden's 115 1/11 – using the American system and excluding all non-sports competitions.

A week later the meet came to a close under the floodlights of the great stadium. As the sun set behind the squat towers of the Marathon Gate, gilding the five entwined metal circles of the Olympic symbol on the parapet on the other side of the stadium, the victors in the final events, the riding contests, received their crowns. This turned out to be a somewhat tedious affair since most of the winners were German so that both their national anthems had to be sung over and over again.

Finally a signal gun boomed in the distance and the tall bell tower on the horizon sprang into life. Massed trumpets beneath the white-clad choir sounded a fanfare; a rocket flashed into the sky and one after the other the searchlights around the stadium beamed out in a great circle. For a moment they shone straight up into the sky, then gradually dropped and converged so that they formed a tent of white above the stadium. Then as

Searchlights form a dome of light over the Stadium in one of the spectacles on the last night

the long fanfare of trumpets ended the head of the procession of nations appeared in the Marathon Gate. The augmented Berlin Philharmonic burst into a parade march as they appeared and formed a line facing the Führer's box. This time their order was reversed, with Germany coming first and Greece bringing up the rear. Count Bailler-Latour officially closed the games and the orchestra and chorus broke into Beethoven's hymn 'The Flame Dies', punctuated by the sound of cannon in the distance firing a last salute. Fifty-one tall white-uniformed girls advanced two by two bearing small laurel wreaths which they placed on each flag. Then as the choir and orchestra began a new melody, 'Farewell to the Flag' by Paul Hoeffer, six bluejackets slowly lowered the Olympic Flag.

The Olympic Flame slowly died away, the bright lights above the stadium dimmed and for a full minute all present stood in silence until presently the sailors gathered up the Olympic Flag and took it to William May Garland who, as the representative of the Mayor of Los Angeles, presented it in turn to Mayor Lippert of Berlin. Three flags were simultaneously raised above the scoreboard; Greece, the originators of the Games, in the center, Germany, the host nation, on the left and the flag of Japan, the next host, on the right. Through the loudspeakers came a clear voice crying 'I call the youth of the world to Tokyo!' No one could foresee that in 1940 Japan would be too busy fighting in China, and the European countries too busy fighting among themselves to spare a thought for the Olympic Games, as everyone rose throughout the stadium and, linking hands in a typical burst of German sentiment, joined in the last verse of the farewell song, 'The Games are Ended'. With this the XI Olympics, the records they set and the names they emblazoned upon the scrolls of sport, passed into history.

The ceremony left the Germans in

A mass display of precision gymnastics
by German sporting associations

Richard Degener wins the springboard event for America

the stadium still on their feet shouting in a frenzy of patriotic fervor 'Sieg Heil! Sieg Heil!', for Germany had done better than anyone, even her most optimistic sportsmen, had thought possible. She had always been a land of fencers, gymnasts, Graeco-Roman wrestlers and the like, but when she had produced good track men, oarsmen or swimmers they had seemed fated not to be able to make an impression when it counted. So her three field event winners – Hein, Woellke and Stoek – became national heros of quite astounding proportions and were regarded with a mixture of awe and gratitude. Second in public favor came the oarsmen; for the first time Germany had come first in what is generally considered to be a major Olympic competition. But the masculine Third Reich owed much of its success to its women athletes for, except in the swimming pool, German women were consistently better than their rivals in every event. In the track and field competition American and German women captured the same number of Gold Medals, but the German women attained many more second and third places than did their American rivals.

The host nation has some advantage in any Olympic contest since, with minimal travelling expenses, it can afford to enter full teams for all of the minor events. This fact worked in favor of the United States at the Los Angeles Olympics in 1932, but the 'minor sports explanation' of Germany's grand total in 1936 is just only in the sense that in the field of minor sports as whole the Germans always had something to offer and so piled up a great many second and third places. The overall sports picture can perhaps be seen best in a brief summary of the XI Olympics as a whole:

Track and field: America made her greatest showing in twelve years and completely dominated the meet, with

Above : Jack Medica (center) takes the Gold Medal for America in the 400-meter freestyle swimming event. Uto and Makino of Japan were second and third. *Below :* Karl Schwarzmann flies over the bar in a straddle to become the all-round gymnastics champion. The Germans also won the team event

Above : Italians, Hungarians, Frenchmen and Germans – approximately in that order – dominated all the fencing bouts after the first eliminations. *Below :* The German weightlifting team. *Right :* German Gold Medallist Captain Stubbendorf clears the difficult fascine ditch on 'Nurmi', while Captain Ferruzzi (below) of Italy on 'Manola' was forced to withdraw

Above : The Indian field hockey team, victors over the Germans in the final. *Below :* In the cycling events Germany and France battled for the medals, with the Frenchmen winning more than the Germans

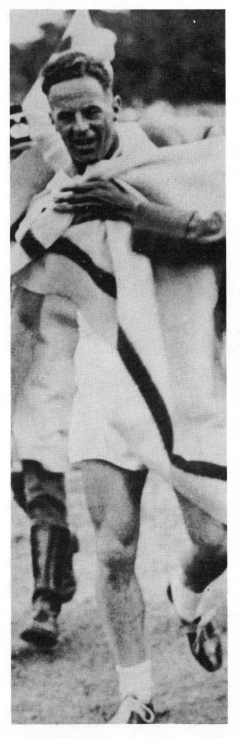

Lieutenant Gotthardt Handrick finishing the 400-meter leg of the modern Pentathlon. He came fourteenth in the run, and although he had been the best in none of the five events, he was the clear victor in the Pentathlon

Jesse Owens the most outstanding athlete. Germany had three Gold Medals, but still finished third behind Finland who dominated the long distance events.

Swimming: the Japanese team consistantly out-swam the Americans, but the latter were saved by their diving squad who managed to collect enough points to put the United States over the top.

Rowing: up until 1936 Germany had won four rowing titles in forty years. Then in one afternoon she took five in a row. Great Britain won the sixth and the United States stole the coveted 8-oared championship from Germany and Italy.

Boxing: Germany took the team title while the 1932 champions from America finished ignominiously in seventh place.

Wrestling: the American team won the free style and Sweden took the Graeco-Roman event.

Basketball: the United States won with ridiculous ease despite the clay-surfaced courts and strange rules they found in Europe.

Gymnastics: in 1932 there had been a close fight between the United States and Italy for the championship. In 1936 no one could even come close to the Germans who had at least one medal in each of the nine events and won six of them outright.

Fencing: Italy set a bewildering pace and came first in both the individual and team events in foils and épée. Hungary won both titles in sabers.

Polo: Argentina was the only first-class team, and no one could halt or even challenge her. Her team's score of 11-0 over Great Britain in the final gives some indication of their overwhelming strength.

Football: football was back on the

Olympic program for the first time in eight years, but Italy's eventual victory was overshadowed by the ugly outbreak in the Austro-Peruvian game.

Equestrian events: the German army easily swept away with all six Gold Medals.

Weightlifting: Germany and Egypt divided the honors, with the United States and France gaining only one winner each.

Field hockey: India was much too good for anyone else and overwhelmed Germany in the final.

Modern pentathlon: Sweden had held the last five pentathlon championships, but in 1936 Germany's Gotthardt Handrick staged a surprise upset. Charles F Leonard of the United States

Participants in a rally for kayak paddlers pass through a lock in one of the many meetings of sports enthusiasts held in Germany during the time of the Olympic Games

took second place.

Yachting: there was no clear-cut division of honors in this competition. Although the Germans scored the most points, Germany, Italy, Great Britain and the Netherlands each won one event. The American team apparently forgot to pull up their anchor, and finished nowhere.

Shooting: Sweden, Norway and Germany each won one event, but Germany had the most medals altogether.

Cycling: Germany strongly challenged the French champions, but did not quite make it. France had two first places and seven places in all; Germany had two firsts as well, but only three places in all.

Field handball: Germany beat Austria in the final to win the championship.

Canoeing: this was a new sport on the Olympic calendar, and Germany's two Gold Medals and total of seven places gave her a tremendous lift to-

A parade of the canoeists. Although the boats were of North American aboriginal invention, enthusiasm for the sport was confined almost entirely to Central Europeans

wards her medal sweep. But Austria won the competition with three firsts and a total of seven places.

No complaints were heard now about Germany's scoring system; using the American method Germany still had a total of 628 3/4 points, followed by the United States with 451 1/3, Italy with 164 13/22, Hungary with 152 15/22, Japan with 151 13/22, Sweden with 146 1/11, Finland with 145 1/4, France with 134 1/2, the Netherlands with 128 5/6 and, in tenth place, Great Britain with 108 1/11 Small wonder then that *Der Angriff*, lapsing into an elegiac mood, said 'We can scarcely contain outselves, for it is truly difficult to endure so much joy . . . every German may be said to have reeled with happiness!'

137

'Olympia' - a Nazi propaganda film?

One of the most exciting things to emerge from the XI Games was a movie, *Olympia*, produced by a young German film maker, Leni Riefenstahl. This film, like its producer, has long been a subject of controversy, being alternately damned as Nazi propaganda and praised as a non-political hymn to physical perfection.

Leni Riefenstahl was born in Berlin on 22nd August 1902. She studied painting and the dance, gaining some success in the latter field before being signed to play in *The Holy Mountain* by Dr Arnold Fanck. Fanck was the originator and leading exponent of the 'mountain film' – an exclusively German phenomenon of the 1920s and 30s which represented an attempt by the German people to find a spiritual shelter, a viable pattern of existence after their battering during the years following the First World War. These extraordinary films marked a new departure for the hitherto studio-bound German cinema; Fanck took his camera on location to obtain incredible documentary shots of glaciers glittering white against a dark sky, or clouds forming mountains above mountains. Many were prompted to take up mountain climbing and it soon became more of a cult than a sport – a strange combination of heroic idealism expressing itself in tourist exploits. After joining Fanck, Leni Riefenstahl – the only girl in a small film company – found herself necessarily involved in all of the phases of film making, and she traces the development of her technique, used to such good effect in *Triumph of the Will* and *Olympia*, to this period. Some of her most notable films at this time were *The White Hell of Piz Palu*, *The White Frenzy*, a pleasing comedy in which she played a girl being initiated into the rites of skiing, and *Avalanche*, in which she braved a perilous ascent in order to save her lover, stranded on the top

Leni Riefenstahl talks to the Reich Sports Minister, Tschammer und Osten

of Mont Blanc. In 1932 Riefenstahl embarked on a career of her own, directing and starring in *The Blue Light*, a film based on an old legend of the Italian Dolomites. Sometime during this year she was introduced to Adolf Hitler and in 1933 she was appointed 'Film Expert to the Nazi Party'. She filmed the Party rally in Nuremburg that year; *Victory of Faith* revealed her masterful editing talent and served as a rehearsal for her most famous propaganda film, *Triumph of the Will*, a documentary of the Nuremburg rally of September 1934.

Hitler himself commissioned Riefenstahl to produce the film, but she was reluctant; she had had trouble with Goebbels over *Victory of Faith* and feared a repetition. So she left town, leaving Walther Ruttman to do the filming. Hitler angrily recalled her and when she returned, finding that Ruttman's plans were not at all what she had had in mind, she decided to do the film after all. She succeeded in making a film which not only illustrated the Convention, but described its significance in a way which was perhaps not intended. The Nazis sought to revive the pageantry and symbolism of Germany's primative past, and *Triumph of the Will* evokes all its savage power and panoply. Speeches played a relatively minor role; the masses were mobilized into a state of ecstacy as they were swept along in continuous well-organized movement. The city was a sea of waving swastika banners, bonfires and torches lit up the night, and the streets echoed continuously with the rhythm of march music. Riefenstahl's cameras incessantly scanned faces, uniforms, legs, arms, faces again; even the buildings seem caught up in the excitement. There was constant panning, tilting up and down – spectators not only saw the feverish constantly-moving world, but

Leni Riefenstahl directing the shooting of *Olympia*, the controversial film of the Games

felt themselves enmeshed in it. *Triumph of the Will*, with its outstanding imagery, such as the two rows of raised arms that converge upon Hitler's car as it moves between them, is certainly an artistic triumph, but as a propaganda vehicle its importance has perhaps been overemphasized: it arouses a feeling not of admiration but of unease in the unbiased mind, due perhaps to the fact that as it proceeds, it gradually becomes more and more divorced from reality and turns into a frightening apparition.

The same techniques that produced this undeniable homage to the Nazi movement were to create an equally effective panegyric to the Olympic Games. Leni Riefenstahl has described the film's theme as *'shönheit'*; a celebration of the grace and beauty of the body, the idea of beauty itself, with no political purpose. The first half of the film links classical antiquity and beauty with contemporary images – tense muscles and strained faces. The use of slow motion, especially in the diving sequences, achieves spell binding effects. Like *Triumph of the Will*, *Olympia* creates an extraordinary atmosphere, well above ordinary life.

With Fanck acting as her consultant, Riefenstahl planned her editing before, not during, the shooting. 'I had the whole thing in my head', she said in a 1965 interview. 'I was like an architect building a house.' Harmony and balance were her keynotes; she strove to alternate tensions, to strengthen the sound if the picture was weak, and vice versa, to move from reality to poetry and back again.

Months ahead of time, cameramen scouted various training fields and all kinds of sports contests to be ready for any emergency and to be able to deal with any incident that might arise; they practised focusing and moving about with their often heavy, cumbersome equipment. This vigorous régime was necessary because several cameras and techniques which were

Left : A member of the Hitler Youth poses in profile – was *Olympia* a Nazi propaganda film, or a non-political hymn to physical perfection ? *Above and below :* Riefenstahl used many new techniques and cameras in this film – miniature cameras, a catapult camera to follow the runners around the track on rails, and (shown here) photographers lying in trenches to film the jumpers

revolutionary at the time had to be used to obtain the results Miss Riefenstahl wanted. Miniature automatic cameras had to be developed, so as not to disturb the athletes' concentration during close-up shots; a 'catapult camera' automatically followed the runners around the track on rails. Photographers lay in trenches to film the jumpers or sat in special towers in the middle of the stadium – the first time such towers were used, though they are common today. Balloons equipped with automatic cameras floated above the field and although only ten metres of every thousand shot turned out to be useable some striking sequences were obtained.

The swimming pool provided the greatest challenge, and the crew, who trained for six months beforehand, responded nobly; they not only used underwater cameras, but attached others to a frame mounted on a little rubber boat that could be pushed around the pool with a pole. Shots were made underwater, at water level and, most difficult of all, with the lens half submerged – another new development. The cameramen themselves performed some startling athletic feats. For example, during the ten-metre dive the cameraman had to dive with the diver, filming him as he fell through the air, underneath the water and as they both rose to the surface; this meant not only holding the focus and adapting to all the light changes, but changing the lens itself at the bottom of the pool (and, incidently, climbing out alive and in one piece). Needless to say, only 5% of that material proved to be of any use.

All of the shooting was done by thirty-three people, including the sequences shot in Greece and during the long trek northwards from Mount Olympus to Berlin. At the Games six cameramen worked in the stadium,

Six cameramen worked in the stadium, eight more filmed the trials, and ten non-professionals roamed through the crowds to get reaction shots

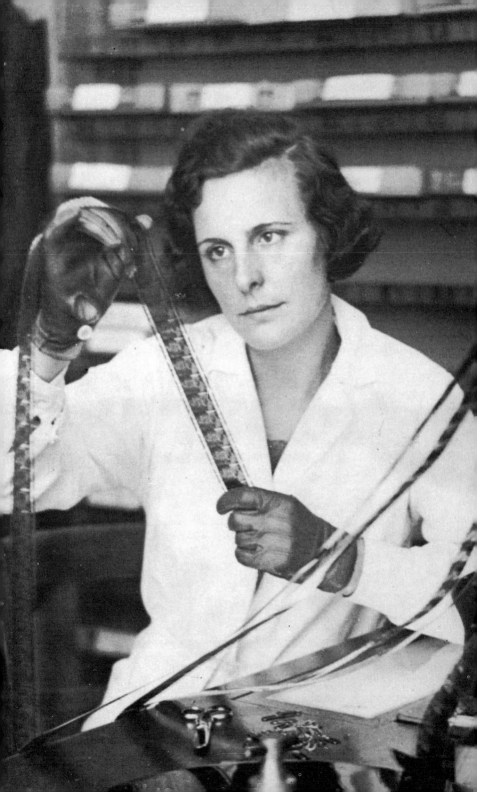

eight more with eight assistants filmed the trials, and ten non-professionals roamed through the crowds to get reaction shots, while Riefenstahl herself darted everywhere supervising, suggesting, even taking a turn on the cameras. But the true establishment of the form came from the editing and this she did alone, literally living in the editing room for a year and a half. All the sound was produced later in the studios and only 30% of the material was ultimately used; finally in 1938 the film that was to become the standard for judging all future sports documentaries was released.

Is *Olympia* a Nazi propaganda film? It is true that in the unexpurgated version some two minutes are devoted to Hitler and the Nazi movement; it is also true that its celebration of sport as a ritual, a heroic superhuman feat, represents an element present in the Nazi philosophy. On the other hand, shots of Jesse Owens and other Negro athletes are treated as lovingly as those of more Nordic types – not exactly a Nazi point of view. It seems clear that, if Leni Riefenstahl had an obsession with health, strength and beauty which may have been peculiarly Germanic, it was not necessarily 'Nazi'. It must be remembered that *Olympia* was commissioned by the IOC, not by Hitler, on the strength of her experience in working on the mountain films: passages in Riefenstahl's books thanking Hitler, Goebbels and Streicher for their help must be taken with a grain of salt in view of the fact that these books were all published during the late 1930s.

Was Leni Riefenstahl a Nazi? There is little doubt that she admired Hitler tremendously – indeed, she does not deny this. 'In 1934, who knew how things would change?', she asked later. 'At that time one believed in something beautiful.' And in another interview, 'I took Hitler for a great and

good man . . . I never dreamed him capable of evil.' She insists, however, that despite their admiration for each other she was never his mistress or anything approaching it, and her descriptions of him quite often sound more like descriptions of a nice man who ran a small business than of a lover or an idol.

Before making both *Triumph of the Will* and *Olympia* she insisted that there be no interference from the Ministry of Propaganda and Hitler agreed to this condition although he was hard put to it at times to keep the resulting feud between Riefenstahl and Goebbels from becoming public. Her word was law in anything to do with pictures at the Olympics, and any press cameraman who put himself where she thought he should not be was tapped on the shoulder by an attendant and handed a pink slip: 'Remove yourself from where you are now – Riefenstahl'. Two pink slips meant permanent removal, by force if necessary, from the stadium. But she still had to contend with constant harrassment during the Games as Goebbels put every petty obstacle he could think of in her way. Once SS men tried to remove her only sound camera from the stadium and she had to spend the entire day standing guard over it; on the fifth day of the Games she was barred from the stadium on his orders and she had to go over his head to gain admittance. When she refused, during the editing, to remove shots of victorious Negro athletes from the final version he made an unsuccessful attempt to block the remainder of her funds. He even carried his vendetta on to the personal level, going so far as to walk out of a party when she entered the room, saying he could not stand being there with a 'non-Aryan' and claiming that she was a Jewess.

In many cases it is well nigh impossible to determine the truth of some of the specific charges against her, since both Riefenstahl and her admirers tend to over-react to charges of fascism and to give different ver-

The editing room, where she lived for a year and a half, finally using only thirty per cent of the film footage

sions of events at different times. For example, a picture appeared in some British papers purporting to show Riefenstahl, clad in a riding habit, 'inspecting' the bodies of some dead Poles in a concentration camp. Her explanation is that she had followed the troops into Poland on her first assignment as a war correspondent and at the time had actively protested to the general in command in an effort to defend the Poles; an inquiry in 1952 acquitted her of collusion in the incident when she produced witnesses to it. Other versions range from a straightforward acceptance of the visual evidence to claims that the picture is not a photograph at all, but a photo-montage made up to discredit her. It is a fact that the year before the war ended her brother was denounced as an anti-Nazi, sent to a punishment battalion and died on the Russian front; her defenders point out that had she been as influential a Nazi as some claim she probably could have prevented it. One of her part-Jewish associates has reported that during the war she gave him 'amazing' assistance in his efforts to secure exemption from the race laws.

When *Olympia* was released in 1938 it won first prize at the Venice Film Festival and the next year a Gold Medal and diploma was commissioned by the IOC (although this was not officially presented until 1948). But by this time most people with any sense could see war coming and, as a prominent figure in Germany, Riefenstahl could not escape their hostility. Her visit to Hollywood in 1939 was a disaster; she was universally and publicly snubbed by everyone in that film community with the sole exception of Walt Disney who believed that her skill as a film-maker entitled her to a polite reception. In 1945 she was detained by the Allies and it was not until 1952, after two trials (by the Americans and by the French) that the charges against her were dropped. But public opinion was still not satisfied; as late as 1965 the British Film Institute was forced to retract an invitation for her to lecture on her work because of pressure from the British film distributors, and it was not until 1970 that her work could be presented in England.

There would seem to be little basis for these unusually virulent objections; Leni Riefenstahl's interviews are not those of an Eichmann trying to rationalize his former political views in the light of present political events. She is not a person for whom the phrase 'I was only following orders' would have any meaning. Rather, what emerges is an extraordinarily singleminded woman for whom only film-making has any reality. She disliked Goebbels because he was mean and deceitful to *her* and disrupted *her* work, not because of his politics. She liked and admired Hitler more because he was kind to her and gave her money and a free hand in filming than because of his politics, although we shall never know precisely what the balance between the two factors was. It is obvious, however, that war and racial extremism are never so much in her mind as are the inconveniences they caused her as a film-maker; this attitude may be naive, perhaps even reprehensible, but it can scarcely justify all of the accusations she has been subject to since the war.

In 1938 the *Los Angeles Times* said 'as a record of one of the finest contests in the athletic field (*Olympia*) is surprisingly comprehensive and as propaganda for any one country or any one people, its effect is definitely nil'. On a superficial level this is an accurate comment. But it has been pointed out, with some justification, that the film succeeds as a propaganda vehicle precisely because it was not intended as such. The playing down of Nazism in the film proves to be a much more subtle and effective advertisement than all the overwhelming rather heavy-handed techniques employed in *Triumph of the Will* and other Nazi propaganda pieces.

The swimming pool presented Riefenstahl with the greatest challenge. The crew trained for six months beforehand, practicing shots made underwater, at water level, and with the lens half submerged

Aftermath - dissension and disaster

The great gathering at Berlin had been a record-smashing success both for the German organizers and for the competing athletes. Admissions to the Los Angeles Games had been 1,247,580; at Berlin 4,500,000 admission tickets were sold. Receipts from the ticket sales brought in 7,500,000 marks; operating and organizational expenses came to only 6,500,000 marks, so the German Organizing Committee made 1,000,000 marks profit on the Games. Of course, the cost of all the construction and many of the other preliminary items was defrayed by the government; the Committee on its own could never have presented the Games on so lavish a scale. The extent of the Games' appeal to the German people is evidenced by the fact that of the 1,200,000 visitors who flocked to Berlin during those sixteen days only 150,000 were foreigners; all the rest were Germans, including thousands of Strength Through Joy members. They crowded on to the 1,000 special trains to Berlin; each day saw any-

where from 60,000 to 145,000 people entering the city. The GOC alone employed 5,000 people during the course of the Games.

On the athletic side, sixteen Olympic records had been smashed and one equalled, and five new world's records had been set – all this in spite of the excellent Los Angeles Games which saw a good many Olympic records passed and an intervening four-year period which saw twelve world's records broken. The fine performances at the Berlin Games prompted one British commentator to go so far as to predict that 'the four-minute mile and the seven-foot high jump cannot any longer be regarded as

Captain Wolfgang Füerstner, Commandant of the Olympic Village. He died two weeks after the end of the Games in mysterious circumstances. He was one of the last half-Jewish officers to retain active rank, but when the Olympic Village was finished he became expendable and committed suicide

150

impossible, though many may regard either of these performances as extremely improbable.'

Although many sportsmen came away from the Games filled with the warm glow of comradeship and the sense of a job well done, dissention and even disaster followed hard on the heels of the XI Olympiad in many countries.

Tragedy struck in Germany two days after the Games had ended when Captain Wolfgang Füerstner died suddenly in mysterious circumstances. His death was widely reported by foreign correspondents in Germany, but no details were released and no public announcement of his death was made by the authorities for two days. Finally the true facts emerged: Captain Füerstner, the officer who had been in charge of the gargantuan task of constructing and organizing the Olympic Village, had committed suicide. Half-Jewish, he had been one of the last non-Aryan officers to retain his active rank; he was for some years in charge of the army sports program and his work had been so valuable that the War Ministry had developed a blind spot for his questionable antecedents. Perhaps he felt that his excellent work on behalf of the Third Reich would save him from the disgrace of dismissal from the organization that had become his life. Certainly the Olympic Games testified to the high quality of his achievements; the army won more than its share of medals for Germany and praise for the men's sportsmanship was widely publicized throughout Germany. The Olympic Village was an acknowledged triumph; and again the army, under the Captain's direction, had done a magnificent job for the Fatherland. But as far as Captain Füerstner was concerned, once he had completed the crowning achievement of his career he was expendable and became liable to the same fate as had befallen so many of his comrades.

A few weeks before the first athletes arrived in the Olympic Village he was relieved of his command and was made deputy commandant under Baron von und zu Gilsa. He stuck it out to the end, until the task he had been set was completed. But it was impossible to pretend that he could continue in the army any longer and on 18th August, while a self-congratulatory banquet for the GOC and the army was in progress, he sat quietly in his room at home and shot himself. The full details of the circumstances surrounding his death are not known; his own tragedy has been swamped, as were so many others, by the greater tragedy that followed. It is interesting to note that in the official report of the XI Olympiad issued by Germany in 1937, his name is hardly ever mentioned, and never in a context which would reveal the extent of his work towards its success.

There were no suicides in America resulting from the Berlin Games, but there was an inordinate amount of argument and accusation mainly arising from the conduct and policies of the American officials who had accompanied the team. The problem on the whole seemed to be a lack of communication between the officials and the athletes on any level other than that of disciplinary action imposed from above. Even before they left for Germany, American athletes had to sign a number of pledges ranging from a statement of their willingness to observe the Olympic rules to a promise to behave themselves in a manner becoming to an American athlete – which was open to a very wide interpretation. Right from that tension-charged voyage at the beginning, many athletes felt that the officials were being 'petty, aloof and unfair' in their dealings with their charges. They kept pretty much to themselves aboard ship and were reported to have had a very good time; this was not appreciated by the watching athletes who were expected

The US team en route back home

to keep to a strict training schedule. In Berlin some team members resented officials staying in the most expensive hotels, but exercising petty economies in the matter of equipment; some members of the swimming team competed in suits embroidered with the Rising Sun as well as the Stars and Stripes. They had been made up for a meet between the United States and Japan which had never been held, and no one had thought it necessary to get new uniforms or to alter the old ones. The athletes were charged $1.00 per week for laundry – a petty thing which was nevertheless annoying – and members who mislaid their official Olympic team sweatshirts were refused replacements. While officials drove around Berlin in expensive cars, Lawson Robertson was refused permission to hire one.

Jeremiah Mahoney leapt into the discussion, charging Avery Brundage and the other officials with committing grievous errors in handling the United States team. The athletes were, he said, 'Ineffectually led by individuals seeking their own aggrandizement rather than the comfort and success of the teams. From accounts that have reached us from authoritative sources, it appears that our athletes were treated on shipboard in most instances as though they were of an inferior caste, while the officials – whose trips were paid for – basked in the sunshine of their importance and dignity.' Many newspapers agreed with Glenn Cunningham that there had been too much supervision by too many people and with Ralph Metcalfe's opinion that there had been too much official buckpassing. 'A little direction goes a long way,' editorialized the *Christian Science Monitor*. 'This Olympic team ran into more than its share. At times it seemed as though there were as many

Mercedes available for the Olympic officials and Hitler's bodyguard – but not for the competitors

officials in the American delegation as athletes ... Good management should be seen through the good behaviour of its subjects and not heard through the voicing of too many disciplinary decisions. Apart from the fairness of the Committee's decisions, better management would have meant that those particular problems would never have been able to arise.'

After they finished competing at Berlin several athletes were sent on a series of exhibition matches around Europe and this 'barnstorming' provided another grievance, for these tours were badly scheduled and extremely ill-organized. Although the participants were not paid, the AAU did receive a fee and many people felt that the boys were being exploited to provide gold to fill the AAU's coffers.

The hero of the Games, Jesse Owens, was particularly hard hit by this practice. As the track and field competition ended, his continued popularity in Berlin began to grate on his nerves; he was mobbed everywhere he went and after the 400-metre relay he had to change his seat in order to escape from the hordes of autograph seekers. Crowds even laid in wait for him outside the door of Bautzen House in the Olympic Village, and despite his amazing speed it sometimes took him half an hour to get across the threshold.

At first of course he enjoyed being so sought-after and good-naturedly signed autographs left and right. But by the end of his competitions his right arm muscles were getting cramped and his constant companion, coach Larry Snyder, feared that the tension would spread to his speedy legs. To alleviate the strain somewhat other Negroes like Herb Flemming, who were constantly being mistaken for Owens anyway, were given permission to sign his name when asked for autographs. Even so, it was a relief to escape from the crushing throngs in Berlin when, immediately after the track and field competition had ended he was sent to an exhibition match in

Cologne. On the other hand he was in no condition after all he had accomplished to start a road tour, and this is probably why Ralph Metcalfe was able to beat him in the 100-metre event. The next day he was put on a plane for Prague without so much as a single mark in his pocket to pay for his lunch. Other athletes on other tours were similarly treated, finding themselves shunted from pillar to post, missing meals and sleep. At Essen Glenn Cunningham and some of his team mates were so tired they could hardly drag themselves around the track to finish their race. 'There's not one boy on the team . . . nor one underling manager who isn't fed up with the entire proceeding', said Larry Snyder bitterly. 'The boys are merely cattle being shipped about. Such things wouldn't and couldn't occur if greed on the part of the AAU was more easily satiated . . . You wouldn't ask the poorest show troupe to work the way these boys worked immediately after the Games, all without a cent of spending money to brighten an otherwise drab picture.'

Finally Owens rebelled. He was booked for a tour in Sweden and Norway, and he just flatly refused to go. He was tired and he wanted to go home. Jesse Owens was not a trouble-maker nor was he a rebel who resented authority; in fact his father (who may have been exaggerating a bit) described him as 'the kind of respectful boy that white folks down Alabama way really love. I know. He's not smart-alecky.' But the AAU, in a rage, suspended him and put pressure on the college athletic associations to do the same. The colleges flatly refused and amid all the bad feeling began planning a campaign to wrest control of the Olympic organization away from the AAU. For his part, Jesse Owens decided that he was fed up and stated that no matter what happened he would never run for the AAU again. Soon after he got back home he signed a contract with Monty Forkins, who also managed the tap-dancer Bill

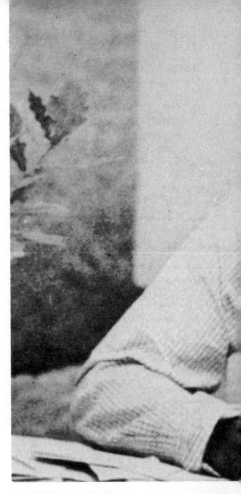

Robinson, and embarked on a career as a band leader; he forgot about his college course and hung up his spikes without any serious regrets.

The reaction in other countries was not quite so violent; in Britain some people were piqued by what they considered to be their team's mediocre performance at Berlin, and there was some agitation for a more consolidated governmental sports program. But it was justly pointed out that Great Britain, not to mention her Commonwealth colleagues, had done far better than Germany had in track and field despite the determination and resources of the latter's truly national sports movement, and the general feeling was that the Games had been

on the whole a success. Throughout the English-speaking world, however, sportsmen felt that the Games were growing too big and were in danger of becoming a circus, with more appearance than character. Jack Lovelock, in a long article in the September issue of *World Sport* expressed the views of most of the athletes:

'Let us give credit . . . to our hosts in Berlin. Nowhere could we have been received with greater courtesy and hospitality and whatever may be thought and said later of the organization and Spirit – sporting, political, propagandist and otherwise – of the whole Festival, all must be impressed with the magnificent efforts of our German rivals and by the courtesy

Jesse Owens, the hero of the Games, signs autographs. Eventually his right arm muscles became cramped and other Negroes (who were constantly being mistaken for Owens anyway) were given permission to sign his name

with which they treated their guests.

'The whole Olympic movement is becoming too grandiose . . . too complicated . . . too over-organized . . . till it is approaching the stage when it will shortly become a stage for the display of ulterior motives . . . no longer for the honour of our countries and the glory of sport but for the furtherance of national ideals and the glorification of the individual victor.'

Personal reactions were on the

whole complimentary, though almost every observer mentioned the ruthless efficiency with which the Games were run; events scheduled to take place at two o'clock started at two and not one minute later. 'The whole organization was one vast machine, a machine which lacked a little the human touch so desirable in international meetings' was the way the official British report put it. The army was very much in evidence to foreign eyes and the preponderance of military uniforms a bit overwhelming. Foreigners felt an eerie atmosphere; perhaps this is why the American team was so strangely anxious to get home afterwards. The officials had assumed on the basis of previous experience that the athletes would want to return by the last possible boat, and indeed most booked passages on the USS *Manhattan*. But at the last minute there was a sudden rush for the *President Roosevelt*, even though it was smaller, less modern and arrived in New York only four days before the *Manhattan*. No one could explain it; the athletes said they liked the food, the country and were treated well, but they just wanted to get home.

From the German point of view the Games were a smashing success. Germany's team had done a marvellous job – in fact by some calculations they had come in first – and it was generally conceded that in the end Germany was better thought of by the people who had visited Berlin because of the Games. Göring, Ribbentrop, and Goebbels gave dazzling parties for the foreign visitors; typical was the lavish reception given by the Propaganda Minister for several thousand people on the Pfeuaninsel, an attractive island in the Havel that had been part of the private property of Kaiser Wilhelm II. A special pontoon bridge had been built to connect the island with the mainland and thirty soldiers were posted beneath it in boats to prevent any vibrations. Ambassadors, generals and admirals, German princes and leading figures in the arts and journalism rubbed shoulders with the stars of sport and top Party members. They entered by passing through a guard of honor formed by dancers dressed as pages holding torches in their hands and dressed in rococo style. Thousands of lights were struck everywhere like giant butterflies; there was an impressive array of food and champagne. Several dance bands played continuously and dancing went on all night; fireworks were let off and a sort of mock warfare was staged which, according to the United States Ambassador, annoyed a great many of the guests.

As the night went on, apparently, some of the tougher Nazi types and less reputable girl pages got a bit out of control, and their uninhibited behaviour displeased some of the more refined guests. Frau Goebbels, wearing a white organdie evening gown, and her husband, clad in a white double-breasted gaberdine suit, presided over an affair which Ambassador Dodd calculated must have cost the government 40,000 marks. This party and others like it helped convince visitors that the government was securely in power, as did the striking unity exhibited by the German people for Hitler throughout the Games. Many businessmen left Berlin very favorably impressed with the whole Nazi set-up and not at all happy with the journalists they met who, they were convinced, had been writing lies about the suppression of churches and so on in the country (despite the fact that the journalists had been in Germany for months or even years while the business men had been there only for a week or so).

We have seen that from the athlete's point of view the XI Olympic Games could not have been better; never before had sportsmen been so well cared for or participated in so great a series of athletic events. But was it worth it? The opponents of the Berlin Games had claimed that par-

ticipation would indicate moral support for the Nazi régime but, due mainly to the strength of the boycott movement, most countries had been at pains to make it clear that this was not the case. On the other hand, many of their predictions came true. They had asserted that the Games would help Germany financially and there is no doubt that they did; the GOC made a good profit, all the tourist-connected industries prospered, and although the government spent a lot of money they gained a lot of desperately-needed foreign currency as well as work for thousands of unemployed workers. The opponents of the Games had also worried about their propaganda value to Germany and here again their fears were certainly justified, for many visitors gained a misleading impression of conditions in Germany as well as of her aims and aspirations, which in turn contributed to a false sense of security in the years immediately preceeding the outbreak

Göring at one of the dazzling parties which he, Goebbels and Ribbentrop gave for the foreign visitors

of the Second World War.

Those in favor of participation believed that politics should have no place in sport. After 1936 this question became largely irrelevant; politics and sport were linked from then on, whether for good or ill. And their opinion that international sport promotes international good will and understanding seems to have been based more in hope than in fact; about the only contribution in this regard that the 1936 Games had to offer was that they provided the setting for Rudolph Hess to meet the Duke of Hamilton – an incident which led to Hess's abortive 'peace mission' to Scotland in 1941. In short, the XI Olympic Games seem to have contributed more to international *mis*-understanding than to the peace of the world and the furtherance of international sportsmanship.

Bibliography

Berlin Diary by William L Shirer (Simon & Schuster, New York)
From Caligari to Hitler by Siegfried Kracauer (Princeton University Press)
Goebbels and National Socialist Propaganda by Ernest K Bramsted (Cresset
  Press, London. Michigan State University Press)
Nazi Culture by George L Mosse, ed (Grosset & Dunlap, New York. W H Allen,
  London)
The Rise and Fall of the Third Reich by William L Shirer (Penguin)
The Story of the Olympic Games by John Kieran and Arthur Daley (New York
  1948)